eco
chic

eco
chic

The savvy shopper's
guide to ethical fashion

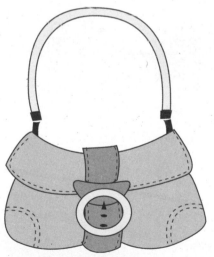

Matilda Lee

Foreword by Katharine Hamnett

To Saso

An Hachette Livre UK Company

First published in Great Britain in 2007 by
Gaia, a division of Octopus Publishing Group Ltd
2–4 Heron Quays, London E14 4JP
www.octopusbooks.co.uk

Research by Laura Sevier

ISBN 978-1-85675-289-3

A CIP catalogue record for this book is available from the British Library

Printed and bound in Italy

Printed on Cyclus Offset, a 100 per cent recycled paper

10 9 8 7 6 5 4 3 2 1

Contents

Foreword

We have to feed ourselves, shelter ourselves and clothe ourselves. Clothing is the third or fourth largest industry in the world. It employs a sixth of the world's population. Consumer research shows that there is an enormous unprecedented surge in consumer concern about who makes the clothes, how they are treated and how the manufacturing process affects the environment. This concern has grown to such an extent that demand for fairly traded goods will soon exceed supply in some areas.

A recent consumer poll showed that 90 per cent of respondents do not want goods made with child labour, 85 per cent do not want goods with sweated labour, 50 per cent do not want goods that damage the environment. Retailing takes very seriously any research that shows consumer opinions above 30 per cent.

Given that marketing has been defined as giving people what they want, a moral imperative to produce goods cleanly, treat workers well and pay above living wages has now become an economic imperative. Yet there is a widespread lack of understanding of these issues.

This book is a must-read for all – clothing manufacturers and retailers interested in long-term business survival as well as consumers who wish to be informed so they can make responsible choices and shop with their conscience.

Clothing is a very significant part of what we consume and people are realizing 'how we consume decides the future of the planet'.

Katharine Hamnett

Introduction

'Fashion is not something that exists in dresses only. Fashion is in the sky, in the street, fashion has to do with ideas, the way we live, what is happening.'

Coco Chanel

'Fashion encourages "wants" not "needs" and sits in an uncomfortable partnership with ecology. How can the industry most founded on artifice and perpetual change ever really become a genuine friend of the earth?'

Susannah Handley, fashion writer

A few years ago, hearing the term 'eco fashion' was enough to send the fashion conscious into collective cardiac arrest. Conjuring up images of unflattering sandals and mud-coloured sackcloths, it was best kept within the circle of a select and virtuous few.

Even those of us who tried to live as green a lifestyle as possible, eating organic and local food, and reducing our carbon footprint, had to stop short when it came to 'green' choices for our wardrobes. After all, eating healthier and better-tasting food was one thing – but what, many asked, were the benefits, if any, of wearing organic clothing?

As looking behind labels became a consumer mantra, the fashion industry managed to keep up appearances, following the idea that the less said about the way clothes are made, the better. How could there really ever be a place for ethics in an industry dominated by aesthetics?

As editor of the Green Pages at the *Ecologist* magazine, I cover a range of green lifestyle issues – from food, wine, health, home and energy to parenting. Admittedly I approached eco fashion with the same scepticism, until seeing my first 'ethical fashion show' a few years ago convinced me to start an eco-fashion section in the magazine.

I'm very glad I did as, over the last two and a half years I have learnt about the impacts of our addiction to cheap and disposable fast fashion, the toxic soup of chemicals that go into making our clothes, and the carbon emissions associated with our global clothing industry.

Not just that, but the fact that it is an industry directly affecting much of the world's population: cotton provides an income for approximately 1 billion people in 80 countries, according to the FAO (the Food and Agriculture Organization of the United Nations); there are an estimated 100 million garment workers around the world; and in Europe and the US there are hundreds of thousands of people employed in retailing, transporting, marketing and more. What we wear affects us much more than I realized.

During this same period I have had the opportunity to meet many of the designers involved in eco and ethical fashion, to research the issues and engage with retailers and leading lights in the industry. And from the very first ethical fashion show that led me into this area, I now work with London Fashion Week on their ethical fashion exhibition, Estethica, through which I have witnessed just how sophisticated and stylish eco fashion has become.

Its sackcloth image now more or less banished, eco fashion has entire issues of glossy fashion magazines dedicated to it, and famous fashion muses now proudly display their wardrobes' eco credentials. But I feel the real story behind the clothes we wear has never been told in its entirety.

This book aims to tell that story. It is based on research and interviews with people involved in designing, making, promoting, retailing and writing about clothes and fashion. It is meant to be a practical guide as well as an informative exposé. I believe there is no use advising people to change their behaviour unless they know why it is important to do so, so issues are explained without being too technical.

The first four chapters look behind the label of our clothes and address the major problem areas involved in clothes making. As new owners of a garment, we are only one part in a long chain of people and processes that have given the garment a life of its own.

Chapter 1 starts off by looking at the nameless millions who labour to make our clothes. Who and where are they? And who or what is responsible for their being overworked and underpaid?

Chapter 2 peers into the nation's wardrobes and asks how quantity became more important than quality. It looks at what really happens when we throw our clothes 'away' and asks whether disposable fashion is really such a bargain after all.

Chapter 3 discusses how the world's two most dominant fabrics – cotton and polyester – have impacted not only our wardrobes but the wider realms of international economics, politics and society. Both fabrics have gone a long way to creating the unsustainable situation we are in, and an argument is made for how they may become part of the solution and not the problem.

Chapter 4 explores the impacts clothes manufacturing has on the environment, human health and animal welfare. Factory workers, retail-floor staff, and at times we the consumers, may be exposed to nasty chemicals from clothes. And as fashions have changed, so has the climate and clothing's carbon footprint. This is discussed, as well as how clothing has contributed to species extinction.

In the second half of the book, I present the solutions to the problems raised in the first half. What we as consumers can do, and what others – including designers, retailers and industry insiders – are doing to carve out a sustainable fashion industry.

Chapter 5 starts by arguing that although fashion is notoriously fickle, green and ethical issues have taken root in the industry. The evidence for this is clear: consumer gauges, media coverage and business decisions. One of the most important indicators of how long-lasting these changes will be is whether or not there is a financial case for going green. I argue that sustainability initiatives can positively affect business's bottom line, and equally there are strong financial reasons against doing nothing.

Chapter 6 surveys the fabrics that are set to dominate the clothing landscape in the 21st century, from organic cotton, wool and leather to hemp and alternative synthetics. These, as well as eco dyes, organic printing and the certification standards and labels created to help clean up fashion, are discussed.

How can you tell if your clothes are made in a sweatshop? While there may be no easy answers, Chapter 7 details what retailers are doing to make fashion fair, and what we, as consumers, can do. It also discusses the most stylish Fairtrade brands and the pioneers behind them.

Indeed, certain designers have been critical in transforming what could have been a trend, into a movement for sustainable style. Chapter 8 pays homage to the group of design pioneers who have refused to hide behind their labels and who have been chipping away at the status quo. Be they campaigners, innovators or thinkers – as a whole, through their work and ideas, they've led to a sea change in the world of clothing and fashion.

And while it is one thing for small-scale, independent designers to take up green causes, what about the mass market? Can high-street chains, which cater to hundreds of thousands of price-wary customers, ever really take up ethical or green issues beyond mere window dressing? Chapter 9 tries to answer this question with interviews with Stuart Rose of Marks & Spencer, Peter Simon, chairman of Monsoon, and Claire Hamer, a buyer from Topshop.

Chapter 10 is for anyone who has ever opened up their closet and found that they have 'nothing to wear'. Relieving closet boredom doesn't have to mean rushing out to buy something new – so I detail seven ways to liven up wardrobes by giving old favourites a new lease of life. From accessorizing, to 'no-sew sewing', to charity-shop chic and vintage, greening your wardrobe can also be very creative.

One of the biggest issues with eco/ethical fashion is knowing where to buy it. The Directory at the very back is the culmination of three years of compiling and research. You will know where to get designer wear, basics, jewellery, denim, shoes and more, so keep it in a safe place.

Dressing for success

If we as consumers begin to ask questions of retailers, if retail buyers begin to educate consumers, if designers, with their unrealized power, begin to consider the environmental impact of the fabrics they use and design clothes to last as long as possible, and if retailers begin to be discerning about the collections they buy ... then things will really begin to change.

Knowledge can inspire action. I believe we can now wear the clothes that reflect the changes we want to see.

Chapter 1

The labour behind the labels

S hopping for clothes is an enjoyable, rewarding experience, right? Discovering something that looks good, feels good and, even better, can be bought for a bargain – we shop to reward ourselves in a number of ways. But as new owners of a garment, we are only one part in a long chain of people who have given the garment a life of its own. At the other end of that chain, at the stage when various fabric pieces, zips, cuffs or buttons are sewn into a finished garment, there is someone with a name and a family who is ultimately responsible for what you are buying. Who is that person?

Some shoppers can still be seen, albeit more and more rarely, turning a garment inside out, checking the insides of pockets and carefully inspecting seams. The reason for this is that, as Christa Weil, a vintage-clothing expert, says, 'A garment's true value lies not in its label, but in its workmanship.'[1] An appreciation of workmanship is one way of saying 'thank you' to the person who made our clothes.

More and more often, though, on today's high street, workmanship and craft have been ignored, and what is on offer, and demanded by consumers, are copious amounts of inexpensive clothes. The reason it's all possible is that that person at the beginning of the chain – the one sewing it all together – doesn't have a name or a face, and in many cases may only be known by a machine number. These are the miserable and exploited who work in garment factories.

Long hours, little pay, child labour, hazardous and unsafe working conditions – this was all commonplace in the UK during the Industrial Revolution. But instead of being stamped out with the progressive legislation and social awareness that brought vast improvements to workers' lives, the problems have simply gone overseas. Over the last 35 years, but particularly in the last ten, history has been repeating itself in the poor, underdeveloped countries where most Western clothes are now made.

What really goes on in a sweatshop? Where are they? Who or what is driving down working conditions and who or what is to blame for not improving them? These are the questions this chapter aims to answer.

And as you'll see, in many cases the problems are structural. From buyers' purchasing practices and 'just in time' sourcing, governments racing to the bottom to attract investors by offering a cheap labour force in special export zones, and weak and un-enforced company codes of conduct that make a poor substitute for proper legislation – we simply can't point a finger of blame on one thing. It's the system that's broke.

What this means is that we, as consumers, have to step in. We have a responsibility to consider that 'cheap fashion' comes at a cost far and beyond what we pay at the tills. We can only blame the retailers in so far as they've managed to lull us into a false sense of security and assurance that we can have dirt-cheap, lightning-speed and guilt-free fashions.

If the person who made our next shirt did so without being able to feed their family that evening what does that say about us?

Clothes on speed

'The reality in the fashion business is, right, what's available? I want it quick and I'm not bothered how it gets here.'
Salvatore Pignataro, Traidcraft

Clothing used to be dictated by seasons. A collection was introduced for 'Spring/Summer' and 'Autumn/Winter'. Beginning in the early 1990s, retailers like Gap and Esprit introduced one for each of the four seasons, still within the realms of what the term 'season' actually means – one of the four natural divisions of the year. This then led some retailers to up the stakes and supply six or eight seasons, then even ten to twelve. Today some retailers have 15 seasons every year. Far from actual seasons, our high streets have now become a constantly revolving carousel of new fashions, changing in a matter of weeks.

This can be explained, in part, by the fact that a clothing 'trend' can be kick-started by a simple photograph of Kate Moss or an equivalent celebrity in a particular outfit, or magazines like *Grazia* proclaiming a certain jacket a 'must have'. When this happens, retailers and their sourcing teams know what to do. They embark on a desperate scramble, ringing around their suppliers to see what the mills have on shelves. If a willing supplier is found, they are asked to turn around, say, a hundred thousand glittery tops or minidresses in two to three weeks. Instead of admitting that this would be impossible, suppliers will say, 'Yes of course we can do it.' Both supplier and retailer know the rules of the game.

'A company puts pressure on the supplier to condense the lead time and it's a one-way discussion. It's all about what the buyer wants. Buyers end contracts if lead times can't be met,' says Salvatore Pignataro, UK purchasing and sourcing manager of Traidcraft. Retailers and manufacturers both know what it is that allows them to survive the demands of 'fast fashion' retail: an expendable, underpaid and overworked labour force in poor countries.

'Workers are called by their machine number, never by their names'

'I made blouses and trousers and there was specialization among the workers – some worked on collars, other sleeves, buttons, until the whole garment was put together. For each 100 garments we put together we get $0.05. In order to make $5 a day, we need to produce between 5,000 and 10,000 garments a day. In order to feed your family, you need to leave the house in the early morning, leaving your children at home, and work until late. You are not able to get up from machines and there is no drinking water. You have a 45-minute break, but it is really only 35 minutes as you need to be back at your machines ten minutes early to be ready to work. We want investment BUT with adequate working conditions.'

Noemi Floras Rivas, garment worker in Nicaragua

Noemi speaks calmly and with confidence to a packed conference in London organized by Labour Behind the Label in early March 2007. The audience – design students, high-street retailer representatives, a couple of journalists and labour advocates – listen attentively. The most striking thing about Noemi is that she is considered fortunate: she is employed whereas there is a 60 per cent unemployment rate in Nicaragua. Just as for millions of other workers who find themselves working in sweatshops, the alternatives are considered worse.

Like Noemi, of the estimated 100 million people worldwide who make clothing and textiles, up to 90 per cent are female. Women have less power, money, protection from violence or access to decent employment and therefore make ideal candidates for sweatshop labour conditions. According to Oxfam's estimates, fewer than half the women in Bangladesh's textile and garment export industries have a contract; most have no maternity or health cover; they work on average 80 hours' overtime a month and receive on average only 60–80 per cent of their earnings – the rest is withheld by factory owners for things like rent, water and food; and it's common for women not to get the first month's wage, to keep them working at the same place. Sexual harassment is frequent and those who complain are dismissed.[2]

Garment manufacturing has been on the decline in Europe and the US over the last 15 years. In the EU, employment in the textile industry fell by 1 million to 2.7 million from 1995 to 2005. A further 1 million job losses are anticipated over the next five years.[3] Instead, over the past five to ten years, employment has been concentrated in China, Pakistan, Bangladesh, India, Mexico, Romania, Cambodia and Turkey.[4] More than a quarter of the world's production of clothing and textiles is in China alone. In Bangladesh, Haiti and Cambodia clothing and textiles account for more than 80 per cent of total exports.[5]

The issue of Europe's shrinking textile manufacturing industry was highlighted recently with the closure of Burberry's British factory in Treorchy, Wales. The number of jobs in the Welsh textile manufacturing industry has fallen from 13,000 to fewer than 4,000 since 1991. The Treorchy factory, which employed 300 people, was closed down despite an ongoing celebrity-studded campaign to keep it running. The plant was moved to China – where Burberry could get the 600,000 polo-shirts produced for £4 apiece, instead of the £11 it takes in Wales, making them an extra £2 million in profit, *Observer Magazine* reported.[6] Burberry's chief financial officer, Stacey

Cartwright, said the move was 'sad but inevitable'. With the retail price of the shirt an average £55, this wasn't a question of make-or-break survival for Burberry.[7]

Should we blame Burberry when all across the high street, the average garment industry worker receives just 0.5 per cent of the retail cost of clothes?

The Clean Clothes Campaign say that the choice to move production to China 'does have serious implications, since the ability to join and form unions of their choice is after all a fundamental workers' right and, in the end, without the ability for workers to exercise such a right, code compliance [with various Western labour codes] cannot be sustainable in the long term.'[8]

China's competitiveness is due to its ability to produce at short notice – but this comes as a consequence of women facing 150 hours' overtime per month (the majority of young workers are women), 60 per cent with no written contract, with standard working hours between 10 and 12 and sometimes 15 and 16 hours a day with one or two days off a month.[9] Payment of less than the minimum wage is common and piece-rate wages are usually not enough to cover living costs.[10]

Migrant workers can easily be exploited because they do not have full residency permits within cities – which limits their access to basic services and allows employers to get away with not offering them contracts and, indeed, often not paying them. In 2004 the total amount of wage arrears owed to migrant workers was calculated at almost £400 million.[11]

It is estimated that nine out of ten Chinese companies do not meet national labour standards.[12] It's no wonder then that factories in China's textile and clothing sector are experiencing labour turnover at the rate of 200 per cent a year.

Doing business in China

In *China Blue*, a 2005 documentary directed by Micha X. Peled, sweatshop factory worker Jasmine, 17, dreams of putting a note in the back pocket of a pair of jeans. 'Just wanted you to know who made your jeans – I cut the thread, Orchid put the zipper on and Li Ping sewed them.' This one scene exposes the most striking disconnection between the people who buy clothes and the people who make them. The 'Made in China' label adorns a large part of the West's high-street clothes, but it tells nothing about the millions who labour for our labels and the conditions they work in.

China Blue is a chilling film about how miserable those millions are. To help support her parents, Jasmine leaves her village to join a jeans factory thousands of miles away, and soon finds herself working up to 20-hour days, seven days a week, with one annual vacation, living in a factory dorm where even bare necessities (water, food) are docked out of her pay. Factory owner Mr Lam is a slave driver, but, in the end, is only passing on the pressure – in time, costs and risk – he gets from his Western clients. One scene shows him meeting a UK buyer (who wished to remain anonymous) with whom he strikes a deal for a rush order of jeans for £4.10 per pair. Jasmine experiences her first round-the-clock schedule to fill the order. The order is filled, Mr Lam gets paid, the UK buyer gets his jeans and, just as always, it's the workers who've ultimately paid the price.

Slaves to fashion: child labour

As much as we may be aware of the fact of child labour in the developing world, it still shocks to know the statistics. The ILO estimates that there are 218 million child labourers aged between 5 and 17 worldwide, 126 million of whom are engaged in hazardous work, and 73 million of whom are younger than 10. Many are trapped in forced and slave labour, debt bondage and prostitution.

The rise of the £3 jeans

It was a scandal in the newspapers when, in 2005, £3 jeans started to appear on the rails of Tesco. All the same, Britain's cheapest jeans were selling at 50,000 pairs a week. And Tesco are quite clear about their role in providing these jeans. Spokeswoman Julie McGuckian said, 'The £3 jeans make brilliant workwear for all types of different people, from builders to fashion students, who can try designs and chuck them away if they don't like them.'[13]

An estimated 32 million people shop in UK supermarkets every week, and over £7 out of every £10 spent on groceries in Britain now goes into supermarket tills.[14] Nowadays, however, a trip to top up on milk, bread and bananas is also a chance to grab a pair of skinny jeans or a coloured bootcut model. Ten years ago no one had ever heard of £3 jeans, but today you can find those and all other types of clothing for no more than a tenner at supermarkets.

At the time of writing, Primark offered jeans for £6, Matalan for £10, Asda for £12 and Tesco (men's jeans) for £10. In Britain, this year, we are set to buy some 86 million pairs of jeans – an increase of over 40 per cent in the last five years. Spending on jeans will reach £1.51 billion by the end of 2007. But it's no wonder – the average woman owns eight pairs.

Jeans are one way that supermarkets and other 'value retailers' have carved out their niche in the UK's cheap fashion craze. Clothing sales at supermarkets are growing five times faster than at retailers in the rest of the sector, with Sainsbury's sales increasing by a phenomenal 50 per cent in the last three months of 2006 alone.[15] In the last year (2006) Tesco's clothing range increased sales by 16 per cent; and overall profits for the retailer are at a record high of £2.55 billion.

One in four items of clothing bought in the UK comes from Asda, Tesco, Primark and Matalan, yet only £1 in every £10 that is spent on clothes is spent there.[16] We are currently buying 40 per cent of all our clothes at value retailers, with just 17 per cent of our clothing budget.[17]

Where does your money go when you buy clothes?

Tearfund have broken down the costs that are involved in manufacturing a pair of jeans according to how much each stage gets, based on the retail price:

• The workers: 0.5 per cent

• Cloth and other materials: 13 per cent

• Transport: 11 per cent

- The shop: 50 per cent

- The brand: 25 per cent (covers marketing and other overheads)

- The government: 17.5 per cent VAT

How far have clothing prices gone down?

Women's clothing prices have fallen by a third in ten years, while the 'value' end of the market is booming, doubling in size in just five years to £6 billion of sales in 2005.[18] What was it like shopping 50 years ago?

Mo Tomaney, a fashion industry consultant and a lecturer at Central St Martin's, says:

'In 1949, my mum earned £1.50 a week in a blue-collar job. She had an account with a dressmaker for one-off items of clothing – a dress, a coat, a suit. She would expect to buy a new coat every 8–10 years. She expected to spend £12 on a coat, which was eight times her weekly income. I was still wearing the coat in the 1980s, when I was in my 20s. This might seem like not a lot of money, but her situation in today's equivalent would be a supermarket checkout employee earning £180 a week, and spending £1,440 on a coat.

Everyday clothes came from the 50 shilling shop. My mum would expect to spend today's equivalent of £270 on her 'everyday' clothes in today's equivalent: Topshop. But who spends £270 on anything at Topshop? Would anyone spend

£270 on a coat at Topshop? Is there anything that sells for that much at Topshop?

These were mass-produced clothes – but they were made in the UK; today 90 per cent of clothes sold in the UK are imported from abroad. Of course, there were always knock-offs but it took a season to get them in shops. Communications brought limitations to having more than two seasons a year. To tell factories about design changes, you needed to send telexes and couriers.

Of course retailers wouldn't just increase the number of seasons for the fun of it, but in order to sell more clothes, and the way they've made this possible is to cut the price of clothes.'

Last-minute sourcing

'Supermarket buyers are the worst.'

Fashion industry Insider[19]

Value retailers survive because they have the power to consistently lower prices and they are able to respond to quick changes in consumer trends.

According to ActionAid, suppliers transfer cost losses from supermarkets onto workers because 'raw materials are ordered at the last minute, an increasingly flexible workforce is employed at the last minute, work is subcontracted, and excessive volumes of work are taken on during the "feast" in case there is a "famine" later on'.[20]

In a lot of cases, contracts are not issued, the order is made verbally and in good faith, which means there is no paperwork to trace back either. This gives retailers a number of loopholes to return or not pay when things go wrong. Suppliers have to outsource work to subcontractors when they receive orders that are too big for their normal workforce to fulfil. There's also been a growth of 'full package' companies that can supply quick-time delivery orders to big retailers.[21]

Prof. John Ruggie, UN Special Representative on Business and Human Rights, states:

> 'The comparatively weak negotiating position of suppliers is also a notable underlying cause of non-compliance [with labour rights]. Factories cannot influence the terms of trade such as price, speed, quality or buyer behaviour. Given this inability to provide upward pressure, the compromises that suppliers make to keep or win contracts and to remain competitive are passed down to the workers in the form of unrealistic time frames, low wages, poor working conditions and abuse of workers' rights.'

The emphasis on speedy production has led to fewer large suppliers in the industry – those which can take advantage of economies of scale – and simplifying the number of relationships that must be maintained by retailers. It works as a kind of hourglass – whereby there are big brand names at the top, which then reduce down to a tiny number of brokers who control a lot of factories worldwide. One example is the Taiwanese-owned company PouChen, which controls 25–30 per cent of all trainer production worldwide.[22]

'Made in?'

According to Adam Mansell, of the British Apparel and Textile Confederation, EU law, to which Britain adheres, stipulates that the only information that a clothing label must include is the fibre content. So neither care instructions nor country of origin have to be on the label. This makes it difficult for the consumer to make informed choices. 'The UK used to have a law back in the 70s or 80s when a label had to state where the garment was made. But that law changed when Britain joined the EU. It's an issue that's been talked about for 20 years in Brussels. They've talked about reintroducing compulsory country-of-origin labelling ... but so far there's been no action,' says Adam Mansell.

Retailers' social audits – a halfway house?

Social audits to check working conditions in factories came about in the mid-1990s after a series of high-profile companies came under fire for substandard working conditions in their supply chains. Although the companies – such as Nike, Levi Strauss, Gap and C&A – had adopted codes of conduct that pledged to prevent exploitation and abuse of workers, they were challenged by groups to demonstrate that they actually met the standards they had adopted.[23]

Today, social audits are performed in the tens of thousands by hundreds of brand names or retailers. But according to the Clean Clothes Campaign, 'Social audits cannot, by themselves, create change, they can only produce a "shopping list" of items to be remedied. At the same time, flawed auditing can have the opposite effect by providing a false or incomplete picture of working conditions.'

Research for a Clean Clothes Campaign report found that the vast majority of social audits performed are being made with plenty of advance warning for factory managers so that the effectiveness and value of the audit was thrown into doubt.

A rough estimate by the Clean Clothes Campaign is that there is a total of 200,000–300,000 clothing workplaces in the world today, only 10 per cent of which are audited each year. 'It is also unlikely that in auditing that 10 per cent, that the worst of the rights violations taking place in the industry are coming under scrutiny,' the group's Quick Fix report states.

The main problem is a lack of joined-up thinking on the part of retailers. On the one hand, there are gestures of corporate responsibility, Corporate Social Responsibility (CSR) departments and the like. Many times, however, according to Dan Rees, director of the Ethical Trading Initiative, these have been 'ghettoized' inside companies. Meaning that these people or departments are separated from the mainstream business decisions. So the overall pressure coming from the company to the supplier is 'lower the price', but a lone voice or department within the company will say 'working conditions matter'.

In other words, as Hannah Jones, Nike senior corporate responsibility officer, says, 'There's no point in Nike having 96 monitors on a factory floor day in and day out monitoring overtime, if overtime is being caused way up the supply chain.'[25]

The Spectrum disaster

A testament to how social audits really aren't working is the case of the Spectrum Sweater factory in Bangladesh. Severe abuse and exploitation of workers were taking place; overtime was mandatory; no holidays were permitted if production ran on; sexual harassment was common; unions weren't allowed; minimum wage was less than that set by the government – which was paltry to begin with.

Not only this but the nine-storied Spectrum Sweater factory was a health and safety hazard lacking planning permission and waiting to collapse. Collapse it did, on the night of 11 April 2005, leaving 78 workers dead and 100 others injured. Before the collapse, the Spectrum factory had been audited by French retailer Carrefour and by KarstadtQuelle. It was producing clothes being sold by Zara-Inditex, Cotton group and Wal-Mart, among others.[26]

Where it is likely to happen – 'export processing zones'

Export Processing Zones (EPZs) are 'industrial parks offering tax holidays, duty exemptions, and investment-allowance reductions'. They offer benefit-free, union-free and flexible labour as an incentive to investors – in fact, virtually the only thing that companies need to pay is worker wages.

Writing in 2000, Naomi Klein helped expose EPZs in her book *No Logo*. At the time of her writing, there were around 1,000 EPZs in the world – employing roughly 27 million workers.

Despite the horrid revelation of the conditions at these places, they continue to exist. And not only that – their numbers have expanded: by 2005 there were more than 5,000 of them, employing more than 50 million workers globally. They are a 'fast-spreading phenomenon' according to the International Trade Union Confederation.

EPZs were promoted as a way to help poor economies way back in 1964 when the United Nations Economic and Social Council adopted a resolution endorsing the zones as a means of promoting trade. Now, according to both the World Bank and McKinsey, a leading business consultancy, the incentives EPZs provide rarely work as they set national and provincial governments bidding against each other, giving away many of the gains from trade that were anticipated for workers and for long-term development.[32]

Unions: the only way out

It is estimated that fewer than 10 per cent of garment workers worldwide are unionized. One of the most effective ways that retailers could improve the workers' situation is to encourage collective bargaining and unionization. Yet research suggests that only 15 per cent of audits even take freedom of association into account, which means that although some companies are touting their auditing as a means to improve the workers' situation, one of the biggest issues is overlooked.[33]

Trade union rights represent the minimum standard for workers' rights. There are two:

1 Freedom of Association: the right of workers to form and join representative organization in the workplace.

2 Collective Bargaining: the right of workers to join trade unions without fear of discrimination ... and to have it negotiate the terms and conditions of their employment on their behalf.

At best workers are not informed of their labour rights: 'Very few workers are aware that workplace codes exist, even in workplaces where employers are making significant efforts to put them into practice,' the Ethical Trading Initiative Annual Report 02/03 stated.

At worst, there is a systematic terror campaign to discourage union activity. 'Nearly 10,000 workers around the world were sacked for their trade union involvement in 2005, and almost 1,700 detained. One hundred and fifteen trade unionists were murdered for defending workers' rights,' according to the International Federation of Free Trade Unions.

The worst country in the world for death within unions is Colombia. Recently released figures show that 84 trade unionists were murdered in Colombia in 2006, marking a 20 per cent increase on the number assassinated in 2005. The CUT, Colombia's main union confederation, estimate that since 2002, 500 people have been assassinated. Carlos Rodriguez, president of the CUT, said: 'Since the CUT was founded in 1986, there has been a campaign against trade union activity and more than 3,000 trade unionists have been assassinated. There is no other country in the world where trade unionists suffer such violence.'

This is happening despite the fact that Colombia has ratified several freedom of association and collective bargaining conventions and therefore has to report regularly to the ILO supervisory bodies.

Graham Copp, from Justice for Colombia, a TUC-backed coalition working with the Colombian trade union movement for basic human rights and social justice, said: 'Although most of the murderers have never been identified, figures from the Colombian Commission of Jurists assert that 75 per cent of political assassinations in Colombia are the responsibility of the state, either directly, or through tolerance of the existence of extreme right-wing paramilitary groups.'

With awareness comes responsibility

The one satisfaction in knowing all this is the realization that there is no better time than now to start to make changes. There is a better way and, as a consumer, there is much we can do. One of the first things is to be aware how best to avoid buying clothes that have been made using sweatshop labour. Clothing labels don't even begin to tell the story of how clothes were made, but while you don't need to become a detective before your next shopping trip, there are guideposts and examples to help you decipher the real cost of the clothes you are buying.

In Chapter 7 I discuss the ways in which retailers are banding together to instigate change in their supply chains and what to make of these initiatives; the idea of fair trade and how it is helping to reverse the downward price trend on the high street; what questions to ask of a retailer to persuade them to do more to ensure decent worker conditions; and I profile some of the leading lights in the fashion world who are striving to put ethics into aesthetics.

Chapter 2

Throwaway culture

A light-pink cotton button-down jacket, perfect for a summer's night out, purchased for a song. It seemed like a good idea at the time. But by the time I tried it on at home, its fit, cut and colour weren't right. It spent a year in my closet unworn and another six months in a bundle with other 'unwanteds' until I finally gave it away. While I'm the first to admit to buying clothes that I don't wear, I'm not the last.

The average woman could just about afford a new car with the amount she spends throughout her lifetime on clothes that go unworn. And it's not just our wallets that are taking a hit: the effects of our culture of over-consumption can be felt across the country, and indeed across the globe.

As the prices and the quality of clothes fall, and the amount we buy increases, what to do with cast-offs is a growing problem. Bursting at the seams is one way to describe the current realm of clothing waste.

How did we come to believe in the infallibility of the 'away' within our throwaways? How did quantity become more essential than quality in our nation's wardrobes? And is disposable fashion really such a bargain in the long term? These are the questions this chapter will tackle.

Bargain basement Britain

'You'd be surprised how much it costs to look this cheap.'
Dolly Parton

Lily P. (this is not her real name) has an eye for clothes. Seven hours a day, five days a week, she stands in front of a conveyor belt at the Lawrence M. Barry & Co (LMB) sorting factory in

Canning Town, east London. All day long, a stream of clothes –
from shoes to women's winter jackets, swimming trunks to men's
trousers – pass in front of her after being offloaded from 2-tonne
trucks outside. The conveyor belt moves at over 6 kilometres per
hour, meaning Lily has approximately half a second to judge a
piece of clothing before shifting it into one of an array of
containers stationed within throwing distance. Every hour, Lily
and the 115 other sorting and grading staff at LMB get through
7–8 tonnes of clothes: over a week, approximately 200 tonnes.

Each of the containers has a name: 'women's cotton dresses',
'women's silk nightgowns', 'coloured T-shirts', 'children's
football uniforms'. A container, once full, is wheeled over to a
'baling' machine, squeezed into an airtight pile and bagged up
into 45-kilogram 'baled' packs, then stacked up to be loaded
onto one mega-container, which holds 504 bales, until it leaves
the factory at the end of each day. The clothes have all come
from households within the M25, but their new homes will be
thousands of miles away.

'People didn't throw things away then the way we do now,'
says Michelle Barry. Michelle, a thirty-something, is a proud
member of a third-generation family in the textile reclamation
business. 'My dad always says you only need one suit: you got
married in it, had your first child christened in it and you wore it
to the grave.' Her father, Lawrence, started LMB in 1985 with his
wife, Joy, and before that her grandfather worked in the
'flocking' business, recycling high-quality wool.

LMB tells us a lot about our throwaway society. From the type
and number of clothes we buy, to how we care for and dispose of
them – LMB holds up a mirror to our consumption culture: we
get to see it for what it really is. LMB reflects the ugly cousin of
the fashion industry, in the dark shadows of the glamour and
desirability of the media's portrayal of clothes and fashion. We

need LMB, and companies like it, more and more but, ironically, the way we shop could eventually drive them out of business.

Our love of disposable fashion means that by the time a lot of the clothes reach LMB and similar companies they have passed their 'sell by' date. It's convenient for us to pass on our worn-out, stretched, shrunk or colour-dulled £5 garments to charity, but these clothes won't be given a second lease of life. This has two big impacts. The second-hand trade in clothes loses out financially – as the quality of clothes gets lower and lower. And the disposable-fashion phenomenon means that our clothes have increasing environmental costs.

The 'rag and bone' trade

LMB is the modern incarnation of the nearly 200-year-old 'rag and bone' trade through which textiles were originally recycled. In 1813, Benjamin Law pioneered the process of 'pulling', when woollen textiles were broken down into fibres to be respun into fresh thread. Up until 30 years ago, you could still find a 'rag and bone' man riding from house to house in a horse and cart, ringing a bell, offering to clear households of almost any and all unwanted goods: old clothes, metal appliances, bottles, even string. In the early 20th century, decades before the jostle to dispose of our waste in an environmentally friendly manner, it used to be second nature to reuse, refashion or recycle pretty much everything. Horse hair would be made into mattressing, string would be recycled into the bags that hold oranges. Wool military blankets were especially prized. Made of 100 per cent pure white wool, they could be dyed any colour and sewn to make high-quality jumpers, trousers or skirts. Each item had its worth, and everyone seemed aware of the merits of frugality.

Today, textile recycling is a well-organized, modern industry, with some 300,000 tonnes of clothes sent for recycling or reuse every year in the UK. Textile collection banks are in well-placed drop-off spots – the kerbsides of bustling city centres, supermarkets, schools or other institutions. Run by charities like Oxfam and Scope or by Local Authorities, in many cases the contents are sold to private clients such as LMB for processing.

Today's bric-a-brac – plastic flowers, metal hangers, reading glasses – will be unlikely to end up remade into something else. The reclamation market that once existed for many household goods has simply vanished. In most cases it has been priced out – there is no need for recycled feathers to make feather dusters, because there are new, cheap feathers from China; string bags are now made cheaply and in vast quantities from plastic. And pure wool has been replaced by CAW, or commercially all wool – less sought after as it means it is 70 per cent wool and 30 per cent anything else.

But the clothing reuse market survived and evolved, making use of skilled labourers. A grader like Lily is expected to sort and grade clothes into approximately 160 different categories. She and her colleagues are trained to be able to tell by a simple touch whether a T-shirt is 100 per cent cotton or not, whether a jumper is made of wool or synthetics, whether a nightdress is silk or a silk-acetate mix. Grades start out simple: either 'reusable' – meaning it can be resold for someone else to wear; or 'recyclable' – it gets turned into wipers or 'flocked'. The industry's term for recycling is when they process a piece of clothing into something new. What we consumers call recycling, they simply call reuse. Clothes go through an additional sorting stage into more considered grades depending on colour, pattern, fabric mix and size. Suddenly a seemingly simple division is actually quite complicated. Lily's honed her skills working at LMB for 12 years. But in one sentence she sums up the second-hand clothing industry's modern affliction: 'There are too many clothes.'

Charity shop chic

The market for resale in the UK simply doesn't match the amount of clothing available. Charity shops do a thriving business, but are only a small part of the story.

TRAID, a high-end second-hand clothing business with eight shops, for example, can sell only a small amount of the clothes donated through their 900 textile banks. The Salvation Army, the country's biggest collector of old clothes, collect an average of 6.5 tonnes per bank per year. Only 1–2 per cent is sold in shops.[1] It is estimated that of the clothing donated to all charitable organizations, the amount that is actually resold in the UK's 8,000 charity shops is as low as 8 per cent. There *are* simply too many unwanted clothes.

The charity shops 'cream' the best of their donated crop, meaning they cherry-pick designer labels and 'like new' garments for their shops. The rest – the 'unwanteds' – used to end up as charitable aid in countries like Rwanda, Kenya and Somalia. In the mid-1980s, this began to change as high demand for cheap second-hand clothing meant that donors could sell the clothes, rather than give them away. It was then that the market became commercialized.[2] The result has been the mushrooming of an industry in the UK in exporting second-hand clothes to developing countries – the value of which has risen dramatically over the last 25 years and globally is worth more than $1 billion (£488 million) a year.

LMB came of age with 'the advent of the affluent eighties [when] people were no longer throwing out clothes because they were old and tatty but because they were out of fashion,' Lawrence Barry says.[3] Their entire business depends on the demand for reusable Western clothes in Africa, Asia and Eastern Europe. In Kenya, for example, clothes are sold to importers who may buy an entire mega-container of 504 bales and in turn resell them to wholesalers, who divide up the bales and sell them on to small retailers at the many travelling markets across sub-Saharan Africa. 'If buttons are missing, if there are stains, or rips, it doesn't get reused; we make sure all the garments sent for reuse are good quality,' Michelle says.

Stitching up the African textile industry?

Reports on the impacts of the second-hand clothing trade in Africa are conflicting.[4] Supporters of the SHC industry point out that:

• The trade creates employment and supports hundreds of thousands of livelihoods in developing countries, for example roughly 2 million associated jobs are being created in Kenya, where over half the population live in dire poverty. Jobs include trading, distributing, transporting, cleaning, repairing, restyling and washing clothes.

• It provides low-cost clothing for people living in poverty although in many sub-Saharan African countries it seems that almost all socio-economic groups are choosing to buy used clothes. It is estimated that one-third of the African population dress in European and US second-hand clothes.

Detractors claim that:

- It hinders domestic textile markets and garment industry development.

- In Senegal, around 1,355 people work in formal-sector textile/clothing industries and an estimated 62,000 in the second-hand clothing industry.

- The number of textile firms in Zambia fell from 140 to 8, and employment in textile manufacturing from 34,000 to 4,000 when the IMF eliminated tariffs on second-hand clothes.[5]

- At the same time, the flood of cheap imports from Asia is one reason for the decline in Africa's domestic textile industries.

'We can't get away with exporting s**t'

Ray Clark, LMB's long-time operations manager, says, 'Twenty-five years ago Africans had a certain name for clothes made in the UK: "Marks & Spencer" – it was synonymous with quality. Most people won't have washing machines at home so the likelihood is that they are washing by hand on rocks. They have to withstand much more wear and tear than we might be used to in the West. Through wash and wear, these clothes would still be expected to last for years. Today, they tell me, "These are not English clothes, the label says 'Made in China'," and they know the quality will be lower. Over the last five years especially, the quality of our clothes has gone right down. Our problem is we can't get away with exporting shit.'

Herein lies the biggest threat to the second-hand clothing industry: the declining quality of our clothes. Less than half the clothes LMB buy from Local Authorities can be exported for reuse. The other half aren't of good enough quality. The only way to deal with them is to process them into something else. Currently 23 per cent is made into cleaning and wiping cloths for industrial use. There are 16 different wiper grades – from linen to denim to coloured and white cotton (the airline industry, for example, has to have white cotton rags to make sure they don't get lost inside the plane's engine). LMB produce 20 tonnes of 'wipers' a week by ripping up fabrics into neatly sized squares. Another 23 per cent goes to flocking – when fibres are pulled apart into single strands and then used as padding in upholstery or insulation. They are one of the few remaining companies set up to do 'flocking'. The other 7 per cent of what LMB receive isn't good for anything, so they pay to send it to landfill.

Alan Wheeler, of the Textile Recycling Association (TRA), a member body representing textile recycling/reclamation companies and charities, can attest to the industry changes resulting in the increase in lower-quality imported clothes, many from the Far East. A 2005 survey of eight European countries, conducted by TRA, estimated that in 2000, around 65 per cent of all clothing/textiles the recycling/reuse industry received was of a good enough quality that the items could be reused again. In 2005, this figure had dropped to around 50 per cent. The Bureau of International Recycling estimates that only around 40 per cent of clothing sent for reclamation in Europe is now suitable for reuse.[6]

Unlike charitable organizations, which have clothes donated to them, LMB pay £60 per tonne for the contents of textile recycling banks run by Local Authorities. Their fleet of trucks pick up clothes directly from the banks and drop them at the Canning Town factory. They therefore have no way of knowing what they are buying. And they don't 'cream' or sort clothes by taking out the best labels. They don't even look at labels – unless it is to double-check the fabric content. So the Dolce & Gabbana shoes are given the same value as an undamaged pair of trainers from Asda/Wal-Mart, providing neither is damaged, stained or too worn out. In fact, the grading system at LMB might seem strange to a Westerner. Trousers, for example, are graded based on whether or not they have a crease down the leg and turn up at the hem (top grade); those that don't, though they might be Paul Smith, are graded lower. The differences in the clothing markets in the UK and Africa are two: one, in Africa they are label blind; and two, they demand clothes that are meant to last.

Alan Wheeler and the staff at LMB are victims of the proverbial disposable-fashion phenomenon – by which clothes reaching their third wear are already falling apart at the seams, stretched, shrunk or dull in colour. We're losing out from both an environmental and an economic point of view. Clothes given a second lease of life are less polluting – they save energy, lessen pressure on virgin resources and reduce the need for landfill space. If everyone in the UK bought one reclaimed woollen garment each year, it would save an average of 1,686 million litres of water and 480 tonnes of chemical dyestuffs.[7]

If an item isn't good enough to be reused it is reprocessed into something else, its new value barely covering the cost of grading, transportation and reprocessing.[8] A 'creamed' crop of high-quality second-hand clothes can reach up to £10,000 per tonne for resale in charity shops. It is much more valuable if a £45 shirt is resold in Oxfam for £10 than if a £3 shirt is reprocessed by LMB into car insulation or window-wiping rags. Charities face the same problems as LMB, but without the same make-or-break financial realities as LMB. 'Our industry might not be around in ten years,' Michelle says.

Make do and mend

During World War II, shopping for clothes was a time-consuming, dispiriting experience – a lot of which was spent in queues. Clothes were in short supply; the amount of clothes people could buy was restricted by the rationing scheme introduced in 1941. Every man, woman and child in Britain was issued with a ration coupon book with a set number of points, which was reduced every time they bought an item of clothing or footwear.[9]

According to a Ministry of Information booklet published in 1944, *British Women at War*:

The housewife has the warm satisfaction of knowing how directly her sacrifices of energy and triumphs of ingenious makeshift contribute to the war such as a saving provided by one additional clothing coupon, which released sufficient labour and raw materials to equip half a million soldiers.

The Make Do and Mend campaign, launched in 1942, was the Board of Trade's major propaganda effort designed to reduce consumption, energy and waste. Posters, leaflets, women's magazines and BBC broadcasts advised women to 'Mend and Make Do to Save Buying New'; 'Clothes carelessness is sabotage'; 'Remake, Mend and Renovate'. The Board of Trade produced a booklet in 1943, *Make Do and Mend*, crammed with information and hints 'intended to help you get the last possible ounce of wear out of your clothes' – from how to make a shirt out of a sheet, or a new coat out of two old ones, to how to save water when washing clothes. It even advised on how to wear them: 'Clothes and footwear should be worn on alternate days as a rest does them good.'

From 'make do and mend' to 'shop till you drop'

Today, standing in front of the plethora of clothing racks at an H&M, with smart-looking, colourful £4 tops staring you in the face, the 'Make Do and Mend' mantra will seem outdated and unnecessary. It is the low-value retailers such as Primark and Matalan that have an ability to turn around 'high' fashion or catwalk trends into cheap copies on the clothing racks in a matter of weeks. Primark is renowned for the uncanny similarity between items on its shelves and recent high-end or designer models. It has twice been taken to court by Monsoon for allegedly ripping off designs.[10] 'The value sector will account for 28.1 per cent of the market in five years and is consolidating into the hands of fewer operators,' according to Data Monitor. Unlike the highly fragmented mainstream clothing market, value clothing is becoming dominated by a handful of players – particularly the retailers Primark, Matalan and Peacock.

This has had a huge impact on how we care for our clothes. Today, less than 2 per cent of what we spend on garments goes to clothing cleaning, repair and hire.[11] It's simply not economical to spend £5 on dry-cleaning or professionally mending a pair of trousers when you could have a new pair for the same price.

But put aside not cherishing our purchases, sometimes they are not even worn. A survey by Churchill Home Insurance found that, on average, women buy 14 items of clothing each year which will never be worn. Over a lifetime, this adds up to £12,810 worth of shoes and clothes per woman never worn.[12]

The social significance of shopping itself has entirely changed. Christopher Breward, head of fashion at the Victoria and Albert Museum says:

> 'I think some historians would argue that shopping, especially for fashionable goods, has been perceived as a leisure activity, at least for metropolitan consumers, since the retail revolution of the late 18th century. Department Stores especially have always set themselves up as attractive destinations and centres for pleasure – along the same lines as tourist resorts. That said, shifting work-patterns, the breaking down of "traditional" family life and a deregulation of shop opening hours from the 1970s onwards have also disrupted the more ordered, seasonal organization of shopping practices, and the turnover of new goods in the shops is now a constant, whereas 30 years ago new lines came in at the start of each fashion season three or four times a year.'

The 'fast fashion' trend will be inculcated to the younger generation through magazines like *Sugar*, aimed at 15-year-olds, which show the high-street goods with 'cost per wear', showing how a top for £20 worn four times is as good as a £5 one worn once.

'Just bin it'

The crisis in the second-hand clothing industry is only one small part of the pie. The clothes that have been dropped off in textile banks, brought into charity shops or retrieved through household collections get a second lease of life, even if it is as a wiping cloth. The vast majority of the clothes we don't want – some 74 per cent of new purchases – end up dying long, slow deaths in the nation's landfills. Three times out of four, our 'unwanteds' go straight in the bin.

Between 2001 and 2005, the number of garments bought per person in the UK increased by over one-third.[13] We are now buying approximately 2.15 million tonnes of new clothing each year. Estimates differ as to how big the problem is – the Department for Environment, Food and Rural Affairs (DEFRA) say 1.1 million tonnes are thrown away in household bins every year, whereas a recent report by the Institute for Manufacturing at Cambridge University put the figure much higher at 1.8 million tonnes. To put it in perspective, a single tonne of textiles fills roughly 200 black bin bags. So imagine 220 million black bin bags and you get an idea of what we throw away every year. According to Wastewatch there are 2 million shoes thrown in rubbish bins in the UK every week.

What does throwing clothes 'away' really mean?

- 'Away' in the case of the UK inevitably means landfill. About 75 per cent of municipal waste is landfilled in the UK, compared to 38 per cent in France and 20 per cent in Germany.[14] Only 7 per cent of waste in Switzerland goes to landfill. Textiles make up between 3 to 5 per cent.[15]

- The major problem with clothing in landfill is that it decomposes very slowly – forming leachate in the process, with the potential to contaminate surface and groundwater sources. In the case of synthetic clothes, decomposition may take hundreds of years.

- Methane gas, a major greenhouse gas and contributor to global warming, is another product of decomposing clothes.[16] One tonne of biodegradable waste (which textiles are classified as) produces between 200 and 400 cubic metres of landfill gas. Waste treatment, including landfill, released nearly 22 per cent of the UK's methane emissions in 2003, about 2 per cent of all greenhouse gas emissions.[17]

- There is evidence of health risks and a higher level of birth defects among populations living near landfills.

- There is also the issue of the EU Landfill Directive, under which the UK needs to reduce landfilled waste to about 14 million tonnes by 2010 and after that to 6 million tonnes by 2020. In 2004/05, 20 million tonnes of household waste were sent to landfill.[18] Current rates of landfill tax, which are low compared to other nations, discourages recycling and composting. Landfill tax is £13 per tonne in the UK but there are plans to increase it to £35 per tonne by 2012, compared to £45 per tonne in the Netherlands.

Bra wars

In the early 20th century, Britain was exporting enough woven material to provide a suit of clothes for almost every man, woman and child alive in the world at the time. Industrialization in Asia and the Pacific rim brought a new hub to clothing manufacturing, and production in the Philippines, Malaysia,

Thailand and Indonesia rose sharply in the mid-1980s. By the end of the 1990s, new players emerged – namely Bangladesh, Sri Lanka, Pakistan, Vietnam and China. Western countries have reacted in an attempt to stop their markets being flooded by cheap imports. Trade barriers and protectionist measures – the most iconic of which is the Multi-Fibre Arrangement (MFA) – were put into place.

The MFA, introduced in 1974, was designed to slow down the pace at which the garment industries of developing countries were built up. Importing countries agreed to quotas that limited imports from developing countries. Bangladesh, as one of the Least Developed Countries (LDCs), was exempt from the MFA and so acquired a new advantage over countries like Hong Kong and South Korea, whose exports were then limited.[19]

The MFA, however, didn't do much to ebb the flow of the clothes trade, which was increasingly reliant on cheap labour and mass production, and came to an end in 2004. Developing countries now account for almost three-quarters of world clothing exports.[20] China dominates the clothing trade – and India follows its lead, being the second largest exporter of textiles.

When China joined the World Trade Organization in 2001, safeguards to protect other members from Chinese exports were put into place. Textile imports from China could be restrained until 2008.

These restraints were put into place in 2005 during the 'bra wars' between China and the EU. This is when Chinese garment imports were held in EU ports for several weeks while a deal on capping the growth in imports of textiles from China (which ended up being at 10 per cent for the next three years) was being reached. Some orders had already been placed and the quota for 2005 already exceeded. A deal was reached allowing half the imports in and counting the other half against the next year's quota.

As of 2008 these import restrictions won't apply.

The 'it bag' that ate the rent

'. . . weird as this may sound, I'm actually against the whole idea of the "it bag". If something's defunct after six months, that, to me, is a bad piece of design.'

Anya Hindmarch, designer of the 'I'm not a plastic bag' runaway hit in the summer of 2007[21]

It 'defines our acquisition-mad cultural moment,' according to the *New York Times*; 'a triumph of marketing,' according to *Marketing Week*; 'it's comforting, useful, ego-boosting, and it doesn't talk back ... the one item of glamour that anyone can have – whether they are old or young, fat or thin,' according to the *Irish Times*. What are they talking about? The 'it bag', for example Fendi's Baguette, Fendi's Spy, Chloe's Paddington, Balenciaga's Twiggy, the Fringe by Prada.

'Because high-street clothes are so good it seems profligate to buy designer clothes. But to invest in an amazing bag somehow feels clever because you can't get that kind of quality from Zara,' says Ellen Hoffman, a lawyer.[22] Indeed, it is much harder for Zara and Topshop to copy a bag than a designer dress.

Bag ladies

Instead of owning one bag, women have a collection – a shopper for day, a clutch for evening, an oversized tote for a long flight, a sleek baguette for an evening out with the girls.[23] Women now buy, on average, three handbags a year compared to one every two years as recently as 2000.[24] A report last year by Mintel found that bag sales in Britain grew 146 per cent in the last five years, with British women now spending £350 million a year on bags.

And these bags don't come cheap. The accessories business, particularly handbags, is the fastest growing sector of the luxury fashion market. Selfridges reported that the average price of its designer bags is £850. It's certainly making money for luxury-goods brands. Leather goods contribute more than 80 per cent of profits at Mulberry and Gucci, and Prada made 63 per cent of its profits in accessories in 2005.

The budget-minded among us – take note: 'it bags' can also be bargain bags. When Kate Moss was pictured carrying Superdrug's Prince's Trust cotton shopper bag, they sold out of its stock of 50,000 bags.

Is disposable fashion really such a bargain?

'Yes!' would be the answer of over a quarter of a million women who bought a £12 military jacket from a value retailer that was the spitting image of a design by Balenciaga without the £1,500 price tag. 'Cheap chic', it can be argued, had arrived after *Vogue* magazine featured the military jacket in 2005. How does fast fare? Seven women shoppers confess:

'I'd rather buy one expensive thing than hundreds of cheap pieces which won't last. I'm often put off buying cheap clothes

because they're full of nylon or polyester although I buy the odd T-shirt as long as it's 100 per cent cotton. The idea behind cheap clothes seems to be about the style of the moment, about being "in fashion", which is a phrase I hate. The style seems to be the most important thing and not the quality! For me, quality and comfort are the most important things. I think vintage is worth going for if it's something unusual and is in good condition. My favourite items are a 1930s dress from a tiny vintage shop in Edinburgh and a pair of flat cowboy boots from the Natural Shoe Store which have lasted five years.'

Lara, actress

'*All high-street clothes seem to die a quick death unless they are hand-washed. I do go for the occasional splurge and buy lots of cheap bargain clothes, but I think a wardrobe should contain staples which are longer-lasting and more expensive – overcoats, black trousers, good jeans … Then fun can be had with cheaper fun items as well as accessories. I'm massively into vintage and thrifting.'*

Mary, fashion stylist

'*I don't often buy cheap bargain clothes because I've made the mistake of buying them and throwing them away shortly after. I've had instances when I've only worn them once or twice and then they've lost their shape and gone bobbly. Now I try to buy quality items instead – hence I'm broke. I recently bought an emerald-green designer jacket that I absolutely love. It broke the bank a bit but it will be passed to my great-grandchildren. I can't say the same for any of the cheaper items I've bought!'*

Rosie, art dealer

'I NEVER buy expensive clothes. I love a bargain even though I'm often disappointed by how they don't tend to look so good after a few washes. Serves me right for being a cheapskate! I don't throw them away, though – I hang onto them. My cupboard is full of gross clothes I bought when I was a teenager.'
Laura, furniture painter and writer

'I have cheap T-shirts I've been wearing for over ten years and while the cut is undeniably worse on some hyper-cheap clothes you can still get years of wear from fast-fashion clothes. I don't understand the desire to throw something away quickly just because it was cheap in the first place – whether you spend £3.99 or £23.99 on a T-shirt, chances are you can make it last.

'It's all about being discerning – minimizing erroneous buys and only buying when you're sure you absolutely love the item you're about to take to the checkout. My most expensive and cherished buy is a pair of knee-high pink suede boots. I was convinced I couldn't afford the high price and it took three trips to the shop to finally part with the money. But I've worn them non-stop for 18 months and got more wear and compliments from them than I ever thought possible – straight men have crossed the room to tell me how great they look. I think they're worth every penny.'
Lucy, journalist

'Most of my clothes I've had for years. I like buying from markets and charity shops – or I buy quite expensive and rarely. I bypass the high street as I don't like cheap cotton and seeing millions of the same clothes on the rail. I prefer finding unique, one-off pieces that I'll keep for ever and become really devoted to. Get into thrifting – you really develop your own eye for style and become more discerning.'
Bay Garnett, fashion stylist and author of *The Cheap Date Guide to Style*

'I am a bit of a Primark addict. I have been guilty of impulse-buying cheap stuff (without trying it on) from Primark that I've never actually worn, but I also have things that have cost me very little that I've worn constantly for years. And I always donate stuff to charity shops or put it in a clothes recycling bin when I'm done with it. I shop mainly on the high street, mainly Primark, New Look and H&M with the odd foray into vintage and designer. I buy new stuff on an almost weekly basis. I work in fashion so it's important that I keep up with what's going on. I can't afford to do that at a high price, so I buy my basics from more expensive places, and my trend-lead stuff from cheap shops with a fast turnover and good catwalk copies.

'I've had stuff from places like New Look that I've washed and worn for years, and I've bought far more expensive stuff that's broken on the first wear. That said, I'm often finding myself sewing buttons back on and fixing hems that have come undone – if you buy cheap stuff it definitely pays to learn how to sew! Obviously, cheaper mass-produced stuff does have more of a tendency to be bad quality, but it's all about finding the one gem among the rubbish. I buy cheap stuff, but I like to think I don't buy cheap-LOOKING stuff!'

Gemma, fashion editor

Creating value in our wardrobes

To me the issue is clear: buying fewer, but longer-lasting items is the way forward. In Chapter 10, I describe how doing this can actually be, well, fun. Relieving closet boredom doesn't have to involve buying something new. From refashioning and 'no sew sewing' to vintage and second-hand chic, to accessorizing, swapping and leasing, and finally – the ultimate – making your own, there are many inspiring ways to give your wardrobe a green makeover. In Chapter 8, I profile the eco designers to look out for when you are in the market for new clothes.

A tale of two fabrics

Throughout history, different fabrics have defined how we dress. In the second half of the 20th century two fabrics have been dominant: cotton – which we have to thank for the ubiquitous denim jeans and T-shirts; and polyester – which gave rise to easy-care clothes and the notorious leisure suit.

Far from impacting on just our wardrobes, though, cotton and polyester have a wider international political, economic and social relevance. They are fabrics that have influenced world trade, the women's liberation movement and even the rise of the modern corporation. They are much more than just the clothes they make up.

Today, we can see that both of these fabrics, in their current form, are holding back the creation of a sustainable clothing industry. Conventional cotton is one of the world's dirtiest crops, and polyester, derived from a fossil fuel, has helped bring about cheap, disposable fashion. As a new chapter to their history begins, the rush is on to define their roles as part of the solution and not the problem.

'Utopian fabrics'

Browsing through half-century's old past editions of *Vogue* magazine – the monthly fashion bible created in 1892 – as I did one rainy afternoon in London's Vogue House library, I came across an extraordinary yet unfamiliar piece of modern fashion history. In among the articles you might expect – covering contemporaneous couture shows, arts and culture – there was something even more particular to the post-war era: the advertisements. Quaint, even funny, but far from slick by modern standards, the ads illustrate the transformations taking hold of women's roles in society, and how these were reflected in what they wore and why.

In the April 1951 edition, for example, one ad pictures a woman with a broad smile holding a tape measure stretched out at arm's length, and the ad reads:

'I've got the shrinkage problem taped! I ask for rayon garments and fabrics with the Calpreta Non-Shrink finish then I can be SURE of these advantages: Can be Safely Washed at Home – Perfect Fit After Washing – No Shrinking – No Stretching – Improved Crease-Recovery.'

Calpreta Non-Shrink also makes fabrics rot-proof against perspiration. Calpreta Non-Shrink is available in Utility and Non-Utility Rayon Cloths, for Garments, Dress Fabrics, Curtains, etc.

Or how about this one from the same issue, in which a young woman clutching a stack of papers is hurriedly opening an office door:

Most white-collar girls spend an evening at home 'getting up' those white collars and blouses. Not so Amanda, the smartest and freshest young thing in the office – she seems to do nothing about it. Her landlady notes that an armful of gossamer garments – blouses among them – get rinsed through at odd moments and are seen on the bath-rail next morning, dry … frills floating, no creases … Mysterious? No – NYLON.

Fabrics rot-proof against perspiration? Hanging clothes to dry on the bath-rail? We're not talking about a low-end mail-order catalogue, this is *Vogue* magazine! Compared to today's fashion ads, where a picture is worth a thousand words, these wordy 'advertorials' seem out of place in such an influential fashion magazine. Clothes were explained, as opposed to selling themselves by virtue of how they looked. Just imagine the latest *Vogue* issue featuring an ad with a supermodel extolling the virtues of a designer 'easy care' sweater. It's, well, a bit unfashionable.

In 1951, fashion was something altogether different. There was a confluence of events that brought the issue of women's dress into the wider realms of politics, the economy and science. Women were entering the workforce in numbers never seen before (giving them new purchasing power), the economy was reviving itself after wartime obliteration, and technology was making big headway in all areas of industry – and, in particular, textiles. Calpreta, nylon and a host of other new fabrics advertised in magazines like *Vogue* had only recently been introduced onto the market. These fabrics revolutionized the way clothes were made, bought and worn. From the origins of these fabrics we can also trace the rise of today's mass-produced clothing we call 'disposable fashion'. The question being asked today is whether polyester and other synthetics can ever be part of a sustainable solution to our clothing consumption.

Stocking wars

What's most striking about the new fashions of the 1950s is that they weren't born in designers' studios with the proverbial muse as inspiration. Instead, for the first time ever, men in white lab suits had become instrumental to the way women dressed. These fabrics were modern man's inventions – created from scientific experiments by huge chemical companies – ones we are still familiar with today: DuPont, Imperial Chemical Industries (ICI), Courtaulds and Dow Chemicals. Advertising in magazines like *Vogue* was a rebranding exercise – from makers of arms and ammunitions to easy-care blouses and dresses. They had just begun to do battle for fashion credibility.

Scientists got halfway there with the invention of rayon, the 'artificial silk', in 1885. Rayon, said to be named after the French word for 'shine', is a semi-synthetic – part chemical, part natural. Natural because it is made from pulped wood. Chemical because it is artificially processed. With its silk-like lustre, rayon did exactly what it was meant to do – provide an artificial alternative to silk. It was used for lingerie but, tellingly, was not seen as having the right qualities to be made into ladies' hosiery.

Next up was nylon, the first major synthetic fibre, 'derived from coal, water and air', announced DuPont's then-vice president, Charles Stine. Nylon was first used for fishing line and toothbrush bristles, but found its fame as women's stockings. In May 1940, the American public got their first glimpse of nylon stockings and 780,000 pairs were sold on the first day.[1] Nylon was light, strong and flame-resistant and, importantly, nylon stockings didn't bag at the ankles. Also, while susceptible to snags, they were less likely than silk to develop into runs.

World War I had taught the US it was vulnerable to blocks in overseas supplies of silk; and it was particularly vulnerable to Japan as the source of 90 per cent of its raw silk imports, 75 per cent of which was used to make stockings.[2,3] As author Susannah Handley puts it, 'Within their purses, housewives held the fate of some of the world's most powerful manufacturing conglomerates, and this must surely have given women their first taste of real economic power.'[4]

The burger and chips of the textile industry

In the mid-1950s another revolutionary fabric came onto the market: polyester. Polyester is man-made by melting and combining two types of oil-derived plastic pellet – the hot mixture is the polymer polyethylene teraphlalate (PET).[5] DuPont patented it in 1931, but did not begin commercial production of PET until 1953, under the name of Dacron.

Why were these fabrics so important? 'Consumers wanted a fashion that would not only match the spirit of youth, but also be affordable,' according to Gertrud Lehnert, author of *The Story of Fashion in the 20th Century*.[6] The fabrics' easy-care properties meant a lessened workload for women, which translated into a liberation from domestic slavery; they were less expensive than other – natural – fabrics, and at the same time they represented the pinnacle of modernity, science and technology.

Permanent pleating, drip-dry, crease-resistant, a 'quick tickle with the iron': these were some of the terms coming into parlance that described the time-saving and efficient wash-and-wear properties of the new fabrics. Convenience was beginning to enter the social sphere as a virtue, and a democratic one at that, appealing to all classes.

Synthetics timeline[7]

Although they came with a multitude of names, synthetic fabrics were made by a handful of petrochemical giants including Courtaulds, DuPont and ICI, Dow, Union Carbide, Rhone Poulenc, Montedison and IG Farben.[8]

• 1920s: rayon, brand name Celanese, manufactured for lingerie. Made by Britain's Courtaulds.

• 1940: nylon stockings presented to the American public. The first year on the market, DuPont sold 64 million pairs.[9]

- 1950s: ICI's Terylene and DuPont's Dacron – the first polyester fibres to go into large-scale production in the UK and in the US. Other polyester brand names include: Eastman's Kodel; Celanese's Fotrel; Trelenka; and Crimplene.

- 1959: Spandex or elastane – invented by DuPont chemist Joseph Shivers. Also known as Lycra – a synthetic elastic – it revolutionized beachwear, giving us light, quick-drying bikinis.

- 1960s: DuPont had invented 31 polyesters and 70 nylons – today there are hundreds.

- 1970s: Lycra came of age in leggings and figure-hugging leotards.

- 1980s: synthetics lost their allure and began to be used mainly in blended fabrics. 'Nylon' removed from clothing labels and replaced by 'polyamide'.

Plastic designers

'It was a risky business making couture garments from these untried chemical fabrics, as *Vogue*'s editor Diana Vreeland found when she sent her designer Elsa Schiaparelli gown to the dry-cleaners: it reverted to an oily sludge when it came into contact with the dry-cleaning fluids and ended up in a bucket.'[10]

Susannah Handley

Because they came out of a lab and not a designer's studio, synthetic fabrics had no design history. In order to sell them, a whole mythology had to be created to stimulate demand. As author Susannah Handley says, 'Selling synthetics is selling the invisible and depends upon the power of seduction, convenience, performance, function, economy and, most of all, luxury.'[11]

There were a few high-end designers working with synthetic fabrics in the 1950s – Nina Ricci, Dior, Balmain and Lanvin dabbled in synthetics.[12] Until British designers began using synthetics in a 'spirit of youth', they were frowned upon and seen as unnatural. Eventually, synthetics became known as 'the fabrics that could make the cheap, short-lived, fun fashions of street style'.[13]

It was really designers catering to the younger end of the market who embraced synthetics. Mary Quant's 'Wet Collection' using PVC, and Dior's 1969 gypsy look are two examples.

By the 1970s, the downsides of synthetics could no longer be ignored. John Travolta might have danced up a storm on the disco floor but imagine how hot, sweaty and static-y he must have felt after a marathon performance in his polyester leisure suit and nylon shirt. Polyester's rise had been rapid, but it became kitsch just as quickly.

Later on, it was the Japanese who revived the polyester industry. Issey Miyake pioneered the use of polyester in modern, high-end fashion. His aim was to create the next jeans or T-shirt of the 21st century. By creating a product that was able to pleat and conform to any body shape, he ensured it could be 'trend free'. Indeed, women in their 80s began wearing his 'Pleats Please' collection, which has horizontal, vertical and diagonal pleats made from polyester jersey, leading it to be named the Octogenarian line.

The mid-1980s saw the advent of microfibres. Finely knitted or woven polyester fabrics, they are weatherproof, warm, soft and, importantly, more able to 'breathe' than the first-generation polyesters.

Polyester and the throwaway society

'Synthetics (and plastics) were the agents behind the obsolescence that lies at the heart of the modern fashion industry – mass-produced garments, made from artificial substances, that can be discarded as casually and as easily as they are purchased.'

Susannah Handley[14]

Synthetic fabrics brought high fashion to the high street. The practice of big retailers like Primark and Asda copying designer catwalk collections with lightning speed is, in fact, nothing new. With the onset of synthetics, chain stores would regularly purchase couture gowns from the Paris shows in order to copy them for the mass market.

Synthetic fabrics made consumers begin to expect more varieties in pattern, texture and prints. Fabric mills began upping their production from three to four fabrics a year, to turning out 20 by the mid-1950s.[15]

In 1979, about 7 million tonnes of polyester were produced. By 2004, annual production had risen to some 30 million tonnes.[16] Meanwhile, between 1990 and 2005, the demand for natural fibres had been approximately constant, at about 20 million tonnes per year. 'In the last 20 years alone, man-made fibres have far outstripped what we have been making by working with nature over thousands of years,' states Abigail Petit of the organic cotton clothier Gossypium.

Polyester is the fabric of cheap, mass-market garments. Over half the world's polyester production is now in China, since the EU and US emissions laws were tightened in 1995 and made it impossible to produce in those countries. The price for polyester is constantly dropping, and once the capital investment in the large polyester fabrication factories has been made, it can be produced relatively cheaply.

Ten new polyester plants have been built in China in the last few years, leading to double-digit production growth.[17] China is the number one exporter of clothes to the EU – its market share grew 80 per cent between 2002 and 2005, and it now supplies 31.5 per cent of the market. Polyester clothes flood the market, but many of them aren't made well and even look cheap.

Polyester is not biodegradable, so everything we've dumped in landfills around the globe will be with us for about another 200 years. And because most polyester is blended with other fabrics, it has become difficult for the garments to be recycled (reprocessed) into something else. What polyester leaves us with is a legacy of cheap fast fashion, the ills of over-consumption, and ever-growing mountains of landfills.

Synthetics and the environment

Synthetic fabrics use up a fair amount of the world's petrochemical stocks, a non-renewable resource.

• Polyester production leads to emissions into both air and water of heavy metals, cobalt and manganese salts, sodium bromide, titanium dioxide, antimony oxide and acetaldehyde.[18]

- Most polyester is manufactured using antimony as a catalyst. Along with being a carcinogen, antimony is toxic to the heart, lungs, liver and skin. Long-term inhalation of antimony trioxide, a by-product of polymer production, can cause chronic bronchitis and emphysema.[19]

- Large amounts of water are used in cooling. Mill waste water is tainted with antimony trioxide, which leaches from polyester fibres during the high-temperature dye process.

- Nylon production emits nitrous oxide, a greenhouse gas with a global warming effect some 200 times larger than carbon dioxide.

Can polyester be green?

What with the looming problem of declining oil reserves, the threat of climate change from our already abundant greenhouse gas emissions, and the threat of overflowing landfills – can synthetics ever really be part of the solution? And can designers help rescue us from our synthetic legacy?

One of the most popular uses of polyester in the form of polyethylene teraphlalate (PET), is plastic drinks bottles. Patagonia, a US-based outdoor clothing label, was the first to use recycled plastic bottles to make a polyester fleece. Since they started, 14 years ago, the recycled fleeces have directed 86 million bottles from landfill. Every British household uses an average 373 plastic bottles a year, only 29 of which are recycled. Some 10–11 per cent of household waste is plastic, according to the British Plastics Federation. Recycling just one plastic bottle can conserve enough energy to light a 60-watt light bulb for 60 hours.

It's part of the consideration of how to lessen the environ-mental impact of synthetic fabrics. 'If the notion of wearing plastic bottles seems odd then people should bear in mind both the bottles and synthetic yarn from which all fleeces are made are derived from the same material – crude oil,' says Simon Lee, founder of Greenpac, a company which reuses waste materials and is producing the recycled fleeces for Marks & Spencer.[20]

Marks & Spencer's own recycled polyester collection, launched in August 2007, includes a school collection of a skirt, boys' trousers, fleece and polo-shirt.

M&S has also trialled staff uniforms and men's fleeces made from recycled drinks bottles – it calculates that with the men's fleeces alone it will reuse 22 million 2-litre bottles, saving 6,000 barrels of oil each year from going into virgin polyester.[21] Making one fleece takes just 11 2-litre plastic bottles. In time, M&S hope to produce all the store's polyester clothing from recycled plastic bottles. If this were rolled out to other retailers and the effect began to snowball, then a real turning point in our use of synthetic fabrics for clothes could take place.

The bottles are sorted, then ground into small flakes in a water bath; the flakes are drained and dried, then melted and squeezed through tiny holes called spinnerets; after solidifying, the product is cut into lengths which are knitted or woven together to make yarn.

Eight per cent of the world's annual oil production goes into making plastics. Making recycled polyester clothes, 'will use much less crude oil than the traditional method of producing polyester, because the oil has already been moulded into plastic,' according to an M&S spokesman.[22]

Cotton: a natural fibre?

'At just eight years old, Modachirou Inoussa already helped his parents in the cotton fields, and 29 July 2000 started as a day like many others. Modachirou had worked hard and ran back to the house feeling thirsty. Finding no drink, he set off to search for his parents. On his way, Modachirou found an empty container, and scooped up some water to drink from a ditch. That evening he did not return home. A village search found his body next to the empty Callisulfan bottle innocently used to quench his thirst.'

Pesticide Action Network[23]

It's likely that Modachirou started out feeling dizzy or nauseous just after drinking from the Callisulfan container. He would have had a terrible headache, and possibly convulsions before he lost consciousness and died. The container he drank from had held a highly toxic pesticide, endosulfan, classed as a pesticide with 'extremely high acute toxicity' by the US Environmental Protection Agency. The question is this: why was a disused container with lethal residues lying out in the open? And why was this substance, obviously so harmful, being used at all?

Endosulfan, the second most widely used cotton insecticide in the world, has been linked to many cases of poisonings, including fatal poisonings, among West African cotton farmers. In the village where Modachirou was from, Malanville, in Benin, a French-speaking West African country, over half the population are dependent on cotton for their livelihoods. They, better than anyone, could tell us cotton is not the natural fibre we believe it to be, but rather one of the world's most lethal and dirtiest crops.

The history of cotton

Cultivated in the Indus River Valley (Pakistan) and South America since 3000 BC, cotton, when it grew naturally, had a colour range of 8 to 12 shades – from beige to red, and even green. Following the Spanish Conquest of Peru in 1532, cotton production of the new Pima and Tanguis strains were given preference over indigenous varieties. After the industrial revolution, commercial cultivation turned towards the white cotton because of the use of synthetic dyes. From then on, breeding of cotton species was for length and whiteness.

There are two major species currently produced, out of a total of 44 of the genus Gossypium:

1 Long – *G. barbadense*, also called Egyptian or Pima cotton, it has a high tensile strength, which means it can be spun into fine yarns – creating a soft, durable and versatile fabric.

2 Medium – *G. hirsutum*, the most commonly cultivated species of cotton, accounting for 95 per cent of the cotton grown and used today.

After picking, the cotton boll needs to be ginned, spun and woven to become fabric.

Pesticide deaths – the hidden truth about cotton

'If just one person dies to make the shirts on our backs – it's too many.'

Lord Peter Melchett, policy director of the Soil Association

There are as many as 100 million households worldwide involved in cotton production. In the vast majority of cases these farmers are part of the rural poor – in many cases they are tending to cotton plots that are between a quarter of a hectare and 2 hectares in size. But it is these small farmers upon whom we rely for the jeans, T-shirts and other cotton garments we wear. Some 60 per cent of the world's cotton is used to make clothes.[24]

For many developing-world cotton farmers, the switch to toxic pesticides was quite recent and occurred only when the corporations that produce them began spreading out their markets to developing countries. In Pakistan, only up to 10 per cent of cotton cropland in the Punjab region was treated with pesticides in 1983, but this had risen to 95–98 per cent by 1991.[25]

Pesticides used on cotton, endosulfan among them, are killing farmers throughout the world. 'People keep asking me how many have died from endosulfan and I can't say – no one can say, that's the biggest problem,' says Damien Sanfilippo, of campaigning group Pesticides Action Network (PAN) UK. Not all cases appear in formal medical records – either because victims aren't sent to hospital, or because ill-trained medical staff attribute cases to malaria and other diseases.

What has been documented is that farmers in the developing world experience 99 per cent of pesticide deaths. According to the World Health Organization, there are 3 million pesticide poisonings every year, causing 20,000 deaths among agricultural workers. According to the International Labour Organization, the fatality figure is much higher at 40,000 deaths among as many as 5 million poisonings.

Farmers escaping death may have to deal with many chronic health problems arising from pesticide use, which many local doctors don't have the training to deal with – especially the insidious reproductive health or sexual dysfunction side effects caused by exposure to pesticides. Farmers still face unpaid working days when they are too sick to work. The ironic thing is that pesticides account for over 50 per cent of the total cost of cotton production.

Why do farmers die of pesticide poisonings? In most cases they have no protective gear; but, even if they do, they are working in temperatures of 40 °C, so it's not realistic to wear it. They do not have the storage facilities specified for the pesticides, and, besides that, as the most expensive thing they own, pesticides are a valued product – to be kept inside homes to prevent theft. Using empty pesticide containers for water or food is common.

'If you complain to companies saying that endosulfan is killing farmers, they respond with claims that proper use and proper storage of endosulfan shouldn't cause any problems. It's a total disregard for the reality of cotton farmers in Africa,' says Damien Sanfilippo.

Pesticide factfile

Pesticides are a group of chemicals that incorporate insecticides, herbicides, fungicides, defoliants and growth regulators. Of these, insecticides are the most toxic. Up until the end of World War II, cotton was predominately 'organic', in the sense that it was grown without the use of chemical pesticides. Pesticides have always been used by farmers to prevent pests ruining harvests, but for about 99 per cent of the history of agriculture, these pesticides were natural substances, not deadly chemicals created in a lab.

• Modern pesticides share a common ancestry with nerve gases. After World War II, the use of neurotoxic chemicals – like DDT – were introduced, mainly because they were seen as a cheaper alternative to labour and machinery.

• There are four major groups of pesticides: organophosphates, carbamates, pyrethroids and organochlorines.

• Some of these chemicals are so lethal that, as in the case of the pesticide aldicarb (a carbamate), a single drop absorbed through the skin can kill an adult. Aldicarb is one of the most commonly used in cotton production – in 26 countries worldwide, including the US.

• The World Health Organization classifies the world's most common cotton pesticides in terms of their toxicity. Deltamethrin and endosulfan are two of the most widely used insecticides. Deltamethrin is classed as a II – a moderately hazardous pesticide; symptoms of poisoning include convulsions leading to paralysis, dermatitis, tremors, vomiting and death due to respiratory failure.[26] Endosulfan is also classed as II – moderately hazardous. Aldicarb, one of the most toxic in global agriculture and the biggest selling cotton pesticide, is classified as Ia – or extremely hazardous. Others used in large volumes include parathion (WHO classification:

'extremely hazardous' Ia); methamodophos (WHO classification: 'highly hazardous' Ib – symptoms of poisoning include shakiness, blurred vision, tightness in the chest, convulsions, coma and cessation of breathing); and alphcypermethrin (WHO classification: 'moderately hazardous' II).

Why aren't they banned?

'Poor African country governments are very susceptible to corporate lobbying. Monsanto is more influential than several African countries combined.'

Damien Sanfilippo, Pesticides Action Network UK.

Cotton production is responsible for the release of $2 billion (£976 million) worth of chemical pesticides each year, within which at least $819 million (£400 million) are considered toxic enough to be classified as hazardous by the World Health Organization.[27] Cotton accounts for 16 per cent of global insecticide releases – more than any other single crop, and 10 per cent of all pesticides. Almost 1 kilogram of hazardous pesticides is applied for every hectare under cotton. The bulk of these chemicals are manufactured by just a handful of multi-national companies, with just seven companies accounting for over 60 per cent of the world market.[28]

You can see, then, that it's not only the well-being of poor farmers that's at stake – it's a multimillion-pound global industry that fights to stay alive. 'The use of endosulfan under present conditions in West African cotton farming households seems at best ill-advised, and at worst irresponsible,' says Barbara Dinham, former director of PAN UK.[29] But because of the sheer force of the multinational companies that produce these pesticides, it is no easy matter to try to get them reviewed, restricted or banned by international authorities. There are currently two major conventions in place that regulate some of the pesticides used on cotton:

1 The 2002 Stockholm Convention on Persistent Organic Pollutants (POPs Convention) bans or severely restricts the production, use, trade and disposal of 12 persistent organic pollutants (chemicals that harm human health and wildlife, do not break down easily in the environment and can accumulate as they move up the food chain), including nine pesticides (DDT being one of them). It has been ratified by 117 nations and went into force in 2004. There are, however, exemptions to the banned chemicals – for example, DDT is used to control mosquitoes that may carry malaria.

2 The Rotterdam Convention on the Prior Informed Consent (PIC Treaty) procedure is a legally binding agreement that came into force in 2004. Under the PIC Treaty, once a chemical has been banned in two or more countries in different regions of the world, it can be added to the PIC list. Currently there are seven widely used pesticides for farming cotton that fall under the treaty. But the treaty is more about information exchange, helping countries with issues relating to the import and export of hazardous chemicals and ensuring the chemicals are properly labelled – it does not promote an end to the sale and use of the chemicals it considers dangerous.[30] In effect, the PIC is simply a list of guidelines. Even if a chemical is listed on the PIC it is still up to individual governments to decide what they do with it – how they regulate it. Take the case of endosulfan. Recently, at a Chemical Review Committee meeting for the PIC Treaty,

endosulfan came one step closer to being listed under the PIC, because chemical experts recommended that politicians should include it on the PIC list in 2008. The Pesticides Action Network, which has been actively highlighting the dangers of endosulfan for the past two decades, can at least claim a small victory. Their report on endosulfan, 'Living with Poison', adds to the research, but, as even PAN will claim, there needs to be more data – the problem with pesticide use is that there isn't enough monitoring.

Denim: the most popular fabric on the planet?

The word 'denim' is thought to derive from the name of a French material, '*serge de Nîmes*', a 'serge' or twill-weave fabric made of silk and wool, from the town of Nîmes in France. Levi Strauss is credited with inventing today's denim jeans, originally sold in California in the 1850s to gold miners, who needed clothes that were strong and did not tear easily.

Denim was dyed from natural indigo plants until the introduction of synthetic dyes at the end of the 19th century. Denim is pre-washed then either stone-washed using pumice stones, or enzyme-washed at high temperatures to fade, soften and pre-shrink the fabric.[31] Denim is no longer made just from cotton, it can be mixed with synthetic materials such as polymide, Lycra, polypropylene, polyester and nylon. 'Denim jeans' can also be made using linen, hemp, wool, silk and cashmere.

Every year brings a new wave of jeans: bootcut, flared, skinny, low-slung, high-waisted, distressed, ripped, embroidered, relaxed-fit, black jeans, grey jeans, red jeans, purple jeans, designer-label jeans, supermarket jeans, and now 'eco' jeans made from hemp or organic cotton . . .

The jeans boom

- In 2007 we are set to buy 86 million pairs of jeans – an increase of more than 40 per cent in the last five years.

- Jeans sales are expected to hit £1.51 billion by the end of 2007. By 2012 they are predicted to rise a further 38 per cent to hit the £2.1 billion mark. The current estimated worth of the UK's denim market is £1.3 billion.

Cheap jeans

- Sales of stores' cheaper own-label designs rocketed by 41 per cent between 2004 and 2006 to grab a 24 per cent share of the total British jeans market.

- Supermarkets are selling jeans for less than a fiver; M&S's cheapest pair is £9.50.

- 50,000 pairs of jeans are sold by Tesco each week.

- 12,000 pairs of Baxter jeans are sold each week in Topshop.

Trading unfair: how the deal for farmers got so bad

'We have a responsibility for the impacts of our consumption.'

Simon Ferrigno, Organic Exchange

Alongside all other injustices the African and developing-world cotton farmers face, there is the scandal of US subsidies. It's impossible to minimize the impact the unfair trading system has on the millions of cotton farmers in the developing world. The US's 25,000 cotton farmers get the equivalent of $150,000 (about £74,000) each in subsidies – but they represent less than 1 per cent of the world's farmers.

In 2001/02 cotton prices fell to their lowest level since the Great Depression of the 1930s: $0.92 (£0.45) per kilogram. US producers currently receive about $4.2 billion (over £2 billion) in subsidies, equivalent to the total value of the crop.[32] Global cotton prices would be an estimated 15 per cent higher if all subsidies were eliminated.[33]

In the crop year 2002/03, almost 60 per cent of US cotton was dumped on the global market (39 per cent of total global exports); this figure rose to 76 per cent in 2003/04. What's more, these subsidies are concentrated among the biggest agri-businesses – in 2004 the top ten recipients received 61 per cent of all cotton subsidies – putting paid to the idea that subsidies are there to help small family farms survive.[34]

Brazil took the issue of US cotton subsidies to the World Trade Organization in 2002, with a formal complaint arguing that they depressed world prices and were injurious to Brazilian cotton growers. In March 2005, the WTO Dispute Settlement Body agreed that they did have a price-suppressing effect (approximately 4 per cent), which undermined the value of cotton for all producers. Since the ruling, however, the US has done little to reform their subsidy programme.

Cotton farming's environmental impact

The world area used for cotton cultivation is estimated to be between 30 and 35 million hectares – which hasn't fluctuated much since the 1950s. In that time, though, the output on this land has nearly tripled. What impact has this had on the environment?

- Reduced soil fertility: through the constant application of pesticides, the soil essentially dies, losing all its vital organisms and becoming almost entirely reliant on artificial fertilizers to make the cotton grow.

- Soil salinization: salty earth from irrigated cotton production causes degradation and eventual abandonment of otherwise productive land. Estimates indicate that in six leading cotton-producing countries, between 12 and 36 per cent of the irrigated area is damaged through salinization.

- Water mismanagement: the Aral Sea – once the world's fourth largest inland body of water – is now reduced to just 15 per cent of its former volume. Diverting water from the Aral for cotton production in the Central Asian country of Uzbekistan has led to the disappearance of the sea's 24 species of native fish, including the sturgeon, the drying-out of wetlands, and the creation of tens of thousands of environmental refugees as livelihoods centred around the

Aral's rich fish stocks have been destroyed.[35] The worst part is that up to 60 per cent of the water diverted from the Aral never reaches the cotton fields as it is lost in the decaying irrigation network.

• Pest resistance: when faced with chemical pesticide spraying, pests learn how to become resistant, which results in ever more potent pesticides being applied and a never ending pest-resistant cycle.

• Water pollution: hazardous cotton pesticides are now known to contaminate rivers in the US, India, Pakistan, Uzbekistan, Brazil, Australia, Greece and West Africa.[36] Aldicarb has been detected in the groundwater in 16 US states.[37]

• Risks to biodiversity: pesticides harm soil organisms, migratory species such as insects, birds and mammals, and downstream freshwater species. In 1995, endosulfan-contaminated run-off from cotton fields in Alabama, US, resulted in the death of more than 240,000 fish along a 25-kilometre stretch of river.[38]

Where do we go from here?
Can GM cotton save the world?

GM cotton represents 30 per cent of total world cotton production and 70 per cent of the US's cotton. It is estimated that half of the world's cotton will be GM by 2010. GM and non-GM crops cannot coexist – there are no safe distances between them because wind-blown pollen can transmit genetic character-istics, bringing the risk of cross-contamination.[39]

Far from being the panacea to the woes of small farmers, the Fairtrade Foundation reports that Indian farmers who planted GM cotton reported decreased average yields compared to conventional varieties. They also say there is no evidence that GM cotton has resulted in the promised reduction in herbicide usage. GM seeds can cost up to ten times more than conventional cotton seeds, leading farmers into greater and greater debt.

The Institute of Science in Society reported a trail of 'dead sheep, ill workers and dead villagers' associated with severe toxicity poisoning from GM cotton in Andhra Pradesh, India, in 2006. According to the I-SIS, local shepherds said that their sheep became 'dull' and 'depressed' after grazing on GM cotton crop residues, started coughing with nasal discharges, developed red lesions in the mouth, became bloated, suffered blackish diarrhoea and sometimes passed red urine. Death occurred within five to seven days of grazing. At least 1,820 sheep deaths were recorded in four villages.[40]

21st century fabrics

Organic cotton is always an improvement to conventionally grown cotton. In Chapter 6, I give an account of organic cotton and other planet-friendly fabrics. I also survey the exciting new alternatives to synthetic fabrics and make the case for the revival in UK textile market driven by organic fabrics such as wool, leather and hemp. As a consumer, you'll need to know how to navigate your way around the various certification schemes, so those are also explored.

The Directory on page 219 is meant to enable you to shop with a voice. It's the first port of call for ethical or organic basics, designer wear, jeans, accessories or baby wear. One of the biggest issues in greening your wardrobe is knowing what's out there, so the Directory aims to be a comprehensive, one-stop shopping guide. The Directory also includes a list of the groups campaigning to clean up fashion.

Chapter 4

Fashionably dangerous

Far more important than the latest hem lines or seasonal colour palettes is a part of the clothing industry we don't get to see: clothing production – from dyeing and printing, to finishing, storage and transport.

While they don't sound like headline-grabbing issues, the real story is this: chemical use in these processes is staggering; fashion changes are helping to change the climate; a shawl or handbag can help lead to the extinction of species; and our clothes are polluting the world's precious water, air and soil.

A new era for clothing manufacturing has begun, starting with a spotlight on the impact our clothes have on the environment, human health and animal welfare. It matters – because factory workers, retail staff, and at times we the consumers, may be exposed to nasty chemicals. For everybody's sake, clothing needs to come clean.

The nature of design

'Ultimately things come down to how cheaply they can get it made at the time of production, and how it looks. The ecology of a garment is not considered. Production time is quite tight, we produce 12 collections a year, and I think more time would probably be needed to produce things ecologically and ethically.'

Designer of a major retail chain[1]

For her dissertation for the Textile Design BA Hons course at Chelsea College of Art, Rowan Garland sent a questionnaire to former students now working as designers across the industry. The questions were aimed at gauging how aware textile designers are of the impact the industry has on the environment. Of the 19 replies she received, not *one* of the respondents, nor any of the companies they worked for, had changed their production processes based on environmental concerns, although they did 'recycle their paper'.

This is not to suggest that there aren't clothing designers or retailers who consider the environmental impact of their products, but for the most part, as Kate Fletcher, an eco design consultant, found, 'Designers believe that environmental responsibility is achieved by the specification of natural fibres (particularly cotton) and by making products more durable.'

This is unfortunate given that the process of making clothes – from the fibre to the finished product – involves huge amounts of energy, natural resources and thousands of chemical substances that, at best, are harmless and, at worst, extremely dangerous to human and animal health and the environment. While some clothing companies may even have environmental codes of conduct and 'restricted substances lists' issued to their suppliers, the speed and frequency with which many companies change suppliers means that monitoring and enforcing codes and restrictions requires more dedicated leadership and commitment than many are willing to invest.

The Design Council say that 80 per cent of a product's environmental impact is decided at the design stage. Designers, brands and retailers have a huge responsibility to consumers, to the workers that make their clothes and to the health of the planet. That this responsibility is too often ignored is one of the fashion world's greatest tragedies.

Buyer beware: the chemicals that may be lurking in our clothes

'Clothes are a piece of hazardous waste.'

Prof. Michael Braungart, co-author of *Cradle to Cradle*

There is no need to scaremonger, but we may be risking our health every time we get dressed. When weighing the risks to consumers, it is assumed by retailers and manufacturers (based on safety tests) that the hundreds of substances used in the dyeing, printing and finishing stages of clothes making – all with varying degrees of hazard – do not end up in the final product. While you and I might not be exposed to these substances on a level that would cause serious harm, what is certain is that millions of textile workers worldwide get to touch, ingest, inhale and absorb many of these, in large amounts and on a day-to-day basis.

- Metals such as chrome (used in wool and leather processing), copper, nickel and cobalt can be detected in high concentrations in finished garments (copper concentrations of up to 300 parts per million are not uncommon). Chrome and nickel are known carcinogens and copper and cobalt can be toxic to humans.

- Formaldehyde is used in wrinkle-free, non-iron finishing and also as a fixing agent for cotton and nylon. Formaldehyde is a known irritant to skin and mucous membranes and was recently reclassified as a carcinogen by the World Health Organization. A Danish Environmental Protection Agency study of chemicals in clothes found free-formaldehyde (the quantity that is washed off a fabric and is the total amount that is there) in three out of ten garments tested. Most formaldehyde, if it makes it to the final product, will be washed out after the first wash, but the formaldehyde that is bound chemically (as opposed to 'free') may come out slowly, like every time the garment is ironed. To a consumer, this is somewhat heartening – but it means the greatest levels of exposure are to industry employees, including clothing retail staff.

• PCP (pentachlorophenol), highly toxic and carcinogenic, is used as a preservative and biocide for cotton and viscose so that some of the chemicals applied during weaving don't degrade during storage.[2] Its use is effectively prohibited in the EU.[3] However, it is assumed that it may continue to be used elsewhere.[4]

Dyeing for fashion

'Colour is the first thing to strike the eye, the most definable and dominating aspect of a textile's beauty.'

J. Balfour-Paul

When William Perkin discovered aniline purple (mauveine) in 1856 he unwittingly became the founder of the synthetic dye industry.[5] He probably would have felt dizzy or perhaps nauseous from the amine. Before his invention, the majority of clothes were dyed using natural dyes, including madder and natural indigo; but technological changes, industrialization and population growth brought about a rapid increase in textile production and natural dyes could no longer fulfil the demand for coloured yarn and cloth, especially because of the amount of arable land needed to grow the dyes.

Today, over 700,000 tons of dyestuffs are applied to 40

million tonnes of fabric each year.[6] The Colour Index, the most extensive compendium of dyes and pigments for large-scale coloration purposes, includes 12,000 products under 2,000 generic names. Modern dyes are based on petrochemicals, a non-renewable resource, which makes them inherently unsustainable. Aside from that, there are many concerns to human health and the environment from modern dyes.

- Polyester is exclusively dyed with **disperse dyes**. Small molecules penetrate the fibre and are fixed through a variety of electrostatic interactions. This results in a degree of migration out of the fibre, leading to the high incidence of contact dermatitis associated with disperse dyestuffs. Contact dermatitis and other allergic reactions to these dyes lead to skin rashes, nausea and breathing difficulty. Oeko-tex, the International Association for Research and Testing in the Field of Textile Ecology, identify 21 dyestuffs classified as allergens – all are disperse dyes.

- Dyeing polyester and polyester blends also requires **dye 'carriers'** that aid dye penetration (because they must be dyed at lower temperatures). These are generally toxic, and can be carcinogenic.[7, 8]

- Primarily used to dye cotton, **reactive dyes** did not appear until the 1950s and are now used for almost a quarter of all textiles. These are chemical groups that bind with the garment fibres – and leave up to half the dye in water after dyeing. This goes into waste water as the fabric has to be thoroughly washed to remove the chemicals. At worst, chemicals used in these dyes are hormone-mimicking and harmful to aquatic wildlife.

- Over half of all dyes currently used contain **azo groups**.[9] Made from a nitrogen bond, these give molecules their colour but, under reductive conditions, they can cleave to form amines. Some of these aromatic amines have been shown to be carcinogenic and 22 are effectively prohibited in the EU.[10] Benzidine-based direct dyes were found to be carcinogenic over 30 years ago, and implicated with a history of bladder cancer among textile workers, yet a large number of smaller manufacturers in Asia still produce these dyes.

Goods with prohibited chemicals are still imported into the EU, as not every batch is tested. If, however, a problem is identified in a test, the huge cost of 'empty shelves' – sending back goods and waiting for new ones (while the fashion may have changed) – are pressures that may incline the retailers not to take action.

Water pollution

'Twenty years ago, on the way to college in Wakefield, England, I used to cross the River Calder which would be red one day, yellow the next and blue the day afterwards – depending on what shirts the local clothing factory was making at the time.'

John Mowbray, editor of *EcoTextile News*[11]

Each year, the global textile industry discharges 40,000–50,000 tonnes of dye into rivers and streams.[12] While steps are taken to treat waste in Europe and the US, dyeing mills in countries such as India are far behind. In Tirupur, India, there are 3,000 factories engaged in garment manufacture and export, and between 300 and 400 dyeing houses. The Central Pollution Control Board of India has included the textile industry in its 'hyper-red' category – reserved for the 17 most polluting industries in the country. Some textile mills in India may dispose of untreated waste directly into waterways.

Salt, used to even out dye colour, is discharged in waterways, polluting freshwater courses and making soil too alkaline to support crops.[13]

Also of note is the sheer volume of water used to dye. Richard Blackburn, at the University of Leed's Centre for Technical Textiles, highlights the amount of water used to dye garments. To dye an average T-shirt of 200 grams, 16–20 litres of water would be used.

'About one-half of the world's waste-water problems are linked to the production of textile goods,' say Michael Braungart and William McDonough in 'Transforming the Textile Industry', which can be seen on the Green at Work website: *www.greenatworkmag.com.*

Bleaches and 'optical brighteners'

Optical brighteners are chemicals that reflect light, making your clothes look brighter than they actually are. In clothing manufacturing, they are used after the bleaching process to resolve any colouring unevenness. Many optical brighteners are made using stilbenes. According to Peter Donath, a former chemist and environment, health and safety director at chemicals giant CIBA (now owned by Huntsman), stilbenes are one of the most widely used chemicals, with over 300,000 tonnes a year used in paper manufacturing, detergents and textiles. They are toxic to fish and can cause allergic reactions when in contact with skin that is then exposed to sunlight. At worst, stilbene derivatives are serious endocrine disruptors. There is a lack of sufficient research into the toxic effects of optical brighteners.

Even before garments are dyed, they may be bleached in preparation for dyeing – or bleached if the desired colour is white. The two most common methods of bleaching use chlorine-based bleach, or hydrogen peroxide. Hydrogen peroxide is non-toxic, but costs two to six times more than the chlorine-based process.[14] Chlorine-based bleach is toxic in high concentrations and there are concerns that subsidiary reactions lead to the production of a range of AOX (absorbable organic halogens) including trichloromethane and dioxin precursors.[15] This kind of bleaching is not permitted in Germany and has largely been substituted by other methods throughout the rest of Europe, but the practice is still common worldwide.

Clothing detergents: all washed out?

The UK market for household textile-washing products (fabric conditioners, laundry detergents and stain removers) is worth £1.5 billion.[16] Tablets and washing powders can contain up to 30 per cent phosphates, included to soften the water and help disperse and suspend dirt. When flushed into the waste-water stream, phosphates may promote the growth of green algae, causing eutrophication, which essentially chokes (deprives of oxygen) other water-based organisms. On average, 5 to 10 per cent of phosphate entering the environment in the UK is from detergents and cleaning products (the main contributors being agriculture and human sewage). Sweden, Italy, Germany, Switzerland, Norway, Austria and the Czech Republic have all effectively banned phosphates in household detergents, but not the UK. The World Wildlife Fund recommends that washing liquids contain less than 5 per cent phosphates. See *www.watersense.org.uk*.

Printing

Textile printing involves the application of a colour paste, made up of dye and a thickening agent, and other chemicals onto a fabric. Football and other sports shirts can use a PVC-based plastisol for the printed label area. PVC is not biodegradable and it releases cancer-causing dioxins on combustion. PVC needs phthalates to soften it up and phthalates are suspected sex-change chemicals and suspected carcinogens. Six phthalates are now illegal in certain products in the EU.[17] A commonly used phthalate, di-ethylhexyl phthalate (DEHP), has been shown to cause morphological changes in the testis, including apoptosis, necrosis and loss of spermatogetic cells, resulting in testicular atrophy.[18]

Chemicals and your right to know as a consumer

A new EU law that came into force in June 2007, REACH, regulates chemicals that may be hazardous to our health, many of which are used in the textile manufacturing process.[19] REACH took nearly nine years to develop, and provoked one of the fiercest lobbying battles in EU history, mainly between the chemical industry and health and environmental campaigning groups.

REACH puts the burden of proof onto the producer to show that their chemicals are safe. Information on the vast majority of chemicals on the market is extremely limited, so REACH will require companies to register chemicals and provide information based on health and safety tests.[20]

The EU is currently drawing up a list of 'substances of very high concern' that includes those that cause cancer, are toxic to reproduction, persistent, accumulative in the food chain, and cause 'probable serious effects to humans or the environment'.[21] If importers, producers or downstream users want to use these chemicals they need to get special authorization.

This list will be drawn up over the next two years and companies will be legally required to respond to consumer enquiries about whether any of their products contain any listed chemicals. In the meantime, consumers can put pressure on companies now – by asking for information on the hazardous substances they use. It is surprising how quickly companies can be spurred into action, if they know their business depends on it.

The nasty business of clothing 'finishes'

'I don't wear so many high-street things because I don't like quick finishes on things. I don't like cheapo cotton – it's a bit like fast food for me.'
Bay Garnett, stylist and author of *The Cheap Date Guide to Style*

Chemical finishing is a process of treating clothes with chemicals to give them a desired property. A 'finish' can make a garment softer, shrink resistant, crease resistant, as well as providing 'performance' properties – including antimicrobial agents to prevent sports and undergarments developing odours. Finishing can actually change the chemical composition of a garment and can include:

- **Easy-care properties**: (traditionally using urea and formaldehyde-releasers) water-repellent, crease-resistant, easy-care, easy-to-iron, no-iron properties applied to cellulose and cotton fabrics which wrinkle after washing. They achieve a 'just ironed' appearance for fabrics.

- **Water/dirt/oil repellents**: repellency is obtained with fluoro-carbon finishes, which include perfluorooctanyl sulphonate (PFOS) and perfluorooctanoic acid (PFOA). PFOS has proven health risks and is persistent in the environment. A well-known instance of PFOS was the first-generation Scotchguard – used widely in ski gear and outdoor wear – which was taken off the market. PFOA is a suspected human carcinogen and is also persistent. A major producer, DuPont, has committed to removing PFOA from the market by 2015. There are a range of other fluorinated compounds and salts, but most if not all of them degrade to either PFOS or PFOA.

- **Mothproofing**: (for wool) the commonest chemical is permethrin, which is a nerve agent and toxic to aquatic species.[22]

- **Flame retardants**: can be toxic, non-biodegradable and have suspected or proven health risks depending on exact chemistry.[23] Exposure in the womb to polybrominated diphenolethers (PBDEs) has been associated with abnormal skeletal and brain development in animals.[24] Man-made PBDEs have been observed in arctic wildlife have been observed using archived tissues collected between 1981 and 2002.[25]

Cancer-causing leather?

Just as with the rest of the textile industry, the bulk of the world's $60 billion (£29 billion) leather industry has been transferred to developing countries, mainly in Asia. What this means is that stringent European laws to prevent pollution by production systems are largely ineffective.

The conventional leather-manufacturing process starts off with an initial preservation stage using salts as soon as the skin comes off the animal, and cleaning to remove hair and any unbound proteins in the skin. The next major stage is tanning. At least 90 per cent of the leather worldwide is chrome tanned. Tanning using Chrome III has been carried out for the last 120 years. Chrome crosslinks strands of animal protein, thereby holding them in place and preserving the skin.

Chrome III is perfectly safe; our bodies need traces of it to function. Chrome VI is carcinogenic. Just like when iron rusts, Chrome III can oxidize if it reaches an elevated temperature or moisture; at that stage it will convert into Chrome VI.

How much of the chrome in the tanned leather oxidizes and turns into Chrome VI? According to Dr Andrew Hudson, head of sales and marketing at E-Leather, it's a very small amount, but the reality is that no one knows for sure. He states:

> 'At the British Leather Centre, where I managed the testing laboratory, we analysed leather samples from the Far East and we found that 10 to 15 per cent of those materials, at that time, did contain Chrome VI. Something in the tanning process had encouraged the chrome to oxidize – too high a temperature, leaving it moist for too long, not binding the chrome into the leather.'

Chrome VI will end up in the final leather product and could be in the waste water as well. And that's not the only thing. The problem with tanned leather is that when it goes to landfill there is the fear – the Germans are concerned about this – that over a long period of time it will actually leach Chrome VI. This concern has not yet been properly addressed in the apparel industry, but car manufacturers, such as Volkswagen and Audi and others who use large amounts of leather in their interiors, are concerned about the end of life – and what to do with the leather. As a result, the leather they use is aldehyde tanned, otherwise known as 'wet white' tanned – without using chrome.

And leather purists beware – one of the final stages of leather making, more often than not, is for the leather to get a polyurethane (PU) coating. The polyurethane coating is there to disguise the damage the skins have; when animals scratch themselves, or there is skin irritation, barbed wire, parasitic damage from fleas and tics, all of that will permeate the skin.

Pulling the wool over our eyes

Sheep farming may be part of an idyll of rural life, but in processing wool is actually a highly technical, and potentially toxic, process.

- Sheep dip includes organophosphates, which can cause nerve damage in humans – and sheep farmers especially; or pyrethoids – which are 1,000 times more toxic to aquatic life than organophosphates.
- Manufacturing wool involves harsh scouring agents and bleaches to clean and whiten the wool. Scouring is an energy-intensive process requiring large amounts of hot water loaded with non-ionic detergents (alcohol ethoxylates and alkylphenol ethoxylates) and builders (inorganic salts) to emulsify the wool grease.
- More than 65 per cent of wool is dyed with chromium-complex dyes.[26] Chrome VI salt, which is added to the dyestuff of the fibres, is toxic. Short-term exposure can cause allergic reactions, and at high levels can result in ulceration through

skin contact, and respiratory problems and irritation of the gastrointestinal tract if ingested.[27] Kidney and liver damage has also been reported.[28] Also, it has been shown to accumulate in many aquatic species, particularly in mussels, clams, bivalves and bottom-feeding fish.

Fashionably endangered: the trade in exotic wildlife

There is a huge demand for exotic animal skins and products. In 2006, UK imports of (legally sourced) skins included 12,873 small leather products from the American Alligator; 1,236 whole skins of the Bay Lynx Bobcat; 69,000 whole skins of the Common Rat Snake; and 3,475 whole skins of the Java Rock Python.[29] The global market for mammal furs was estimated at £2.7 billion in 2005.[30]

Yet there is an even more lucrative trade in endangered species, which threatens the survival of certain species. While illegal trade is difficult to measure – a lot of it is done over the internet – and information from seizures is the only way of recording it, in 2003/04, enforcement authorities in the EU made more than 7,000 seizures involving over 3.5 million products from endangered species.

In six UK wildlife-trade prosecutions that occurred between 1996 and 2002, the value of the wildlife products concerned totalled £4,058,000. These cases involved commodities from highly endangered species, such as shahtoosh shawls.[31]

The shahtoosh (Persian for 'king of wools') is the underfur of the Tibetan antelope or chiru. The chiru has a coat of very fine wool that is made into one of the lightest, most expensiveand most sought after wool shawls available, retailing at £21,000.

Three to five chiru die to provide 300–600 grams of wool needed to make a shawl.

In 1900 the chiru population was estimated at 1 million. In1995 it was estimated at fewer than 75,000. The chiru is considered an endangered species by both the IUCN (the World Conservation Union) and CITES (the 'Washington' Convention on International Trade in Endangered Species of Wild Fauna and Flora).[32]

In the UK, shahtoosh smugglers risk up to seven years' imprisonment for import/export offences and five years' imprisonment for the illegal trade in CITES species within the UK.

In May 2000, the UK brought the first successful prosecution for selling shahtoosh in the West.[33] It remains to be seen whether international efforts can save the chiru from an inglorious extinction as a fashion accessory.

Our clothes and our climate

Carbon counting is still an unexplored issue, but one that will grow in importance over the next few years as retailers begin to be audited for their carbon footprint or even offer 'carbon labels' on products. No doubt clothes will be included, as the case for urgent action to reduce carbon emissions permeates all areas of life. We in Britain each cause, on average, 10.79 tonnes of carbon emissions a year; if clothing were accounted for, it would add up to about 10 per cent of our emissions – around 1 tonne. Clothing is responsible for carbon emissions in a number of ways: farming, high-energy manufacturing processes, clothing miles and the 'use' phase.

Farming

Conventional cotton farming, because of its reliance on petrochemical fertilizers, pesticides and herbicides, is very energy intensive. Fertilizers are the largest source of carbon dioxide emissions in agriculture and the single largest source of nitrous oxide emissions for all sectors in the world.

High-energy manufacturing processes

While the demand for natural fibres has been approximately constant, over the last 15 years demand for man-made fibres has nearly doubled. The emissions from the chemical processes used to manufacture and finish garments, especially of man-made fibres, are very high. In the case of a blouse made from viscose, a cellulose-based man-made fibre, 65 per cent of its total 'cradle to grave' energy consumption takes place in the creation of the actual fabric, according to a report by the Institute of Marketing at the University of Cambridge.

Clothing miles

Today, clothing and textiles account for 7 per cent of world exports. A skirt or dress may have travelled around the world once before being purchased. From cotton field, to textile mill, to garment factory in Asia (the majority of textiles are manufactured in South East Asia, China and India), each stage adds to the carbon emissions produced in maintaining our global clothing market.

The 'use' phase

Once purchased, the way an item of clothing is cleaned, cared for and disposed of reflects heavily on its carbon footprint. A typical T-shirt, if washed at 60 °C, tumble dried and ironed, will release 4 kilograms of carbon dioxide emissions during its 'lifetime'. This is equivalent to a 27-kilometre plane flight. In 2006, some 450,000 T-shirts were sold in the UK. If cared for as described, this will result in the production of 1.8 million tonnes of carbon dioxide – more than the annual output of the Republic of Uganda.

The future of design

The best way to avoid chemicals in clothing is to not wear clothing at all, which is, save for a select few, impossible. There will always be chemicals in clothes, and not all of them are harmful. The issue is this: how do we avoid the worst?

While many designers and brands hide behind their labels, in Chapters 8 and 9 I profile a new crop of design retailers who are taking a stand against the worst excesses of the clothing industry. The future of eco design is also gaining speed as many UK design schools are incorporating sustainable design principles into course curricula. In Chapter 5, I detail these courses and talk about the new direction design schools are taking. The leading lights in eco fashion are going a long way to cleaning up fashion.

The rise of eco fashion

How disappointing would it be if by next season eco and ethical fashion suddenly became unfashionable? Let's not kid ourselves: the fashion world is notoriously fickle. Just as fast as it rose – among the industry, the media and consumers – eco fashion could quickly be consigned to the graveyard of fashion trends.

Or not. The case can be made that eco fashion has grown out of being just a trend, and has grown into a movement. The issues have taken root, and for this reason eco fashion represents more than just a cosmetic change within the industry. Consumers have played a key role in creating this movement, and it is through their demands that industry has responded to what was initially considered the 'threat' of green issues. In doing so, however, a further truth has been revealed – that there is a business case for sustainability. While businesses are discovering the ways in which their bottom line is affected by acting on these issues, they have equally come to realize the negative impacts of not acting.

This chapter, and indeed the rest of the second half of the book, will look at the different 'stakeholders' in sustainable fashion. What consumers can and have done to change the system, how designers, retailers, fashion weeks around the world, design schools, and others, have contributed to change that is systemic, and not just cosmetic.

Gauges of ethical consumerism

• The Co-op Bank's Ethical Consumerism Report acts as a barometer of ethical spending in the UK, and its 2006 report shows that in 2005 UK ethical consumerism was worth £29.3 billion, for the first time overtaking the retail market for tobacco and alcohol, which was worth £28 billion.

• Spending on ethical clothing grew by 26 per cent between

2004 and 2005, from £23 million to £29 million, growing at a far greater rate than the general clothing retail market.

- In 2005, 61 per cent of people chose a product or service on the basis of a company's responsible reputation, as opposed to only 51 per cent in 1999. Equally, 55 per cent of people avoided a product or service on the basis of a company's reputation in 2005, up from 44 per cent in 1999.

- Mintel's Green and Ethical Consumer Report 2006 found that one in four (24 per cent) adults is 'Keen to be Green' and is very conscious of, and conscientious about, green and ethical issues, always trying to do more. It also found that the use of child labour was one of the top five consumer concerns – along with recycling, climate change, renewable energy and forest destruction.

- A YouGov survey commissioned by Marks & Spencer shows consumers are thinking more about ethical and health issues when they buy clothing and food. Almost one-third said they had decided not to buy an item of clothing because they felt concerned about where it had come from or under what conditions it had been made; 59 per cent said they had also avoided buying a food product due to similar concerns; 78 per cent said they would like to know more about the way clothes are made, including the conditions in the factories where they are produced, and the use of chemicals in their manufacture.

- Over half (23.1 million) of Britain's consumers think ethical production of the clothes they buy is important, according to the 2006 research from global market information company TNS Worldpanel Fashion. An overwhelming 76 per cent of people feel an end to child labour and sweatshops is a very important driver of ethical production, closely followed by offering producers a fair price (60 per cent) and limiting damage caused to the environment (50 per cent).

- According to Verdict research, consumers are increasingly concerned about ethical standards throughout retailers' supply chains, and retailers need answers to the following questions: What is ethical sourcing? How is it changing?
- MORI research in April 2005 found that half of the British public now recognize the Fairtrade Mark.
- According to Organic Exchange, brand and retail demand for organic cotton products is projected to increase by an average annual rate of 110 per cent between 2006 and 2008, as companies continue to implement long-term commitments to increase the use of organic cotton, and as new brands and retailers enter the market. Estimated global retail sales of organic cotton are projected to grow to $2.6 billion (£1.26 billion) by the end of 2008, reflecting an average annual growth rate of 116 per cent. Manufacturer demand for organic cotton fibre is expected to grow to 99,662 tonnes in 2008, an average annual growth rate of 75 per cent.[1]

Salvation through circulation: the glossies and green fashion

In the beginning, 2004–05 – eons ago in the fashion world – journalists were hard-pressed to organize monthly eco fashion shoots, as the offerings were somewhat slim. Nevertheless magazines such as the *Ecologist, Ethical Consumer, New Consumer* and *Organic Life* have all been regularly covering eco and ethical fashion. Since 2006, once the eco/ethical fashion market became more established, a number of fashion glossies have printed articles and specials, and have featured individual products or designers.

Vogue magazine's October 2006 issue devoted ten pages to ethical clothing, and they have followed it up with occasional articles on the subject. *Vanity Fair*'s first 'Green Issue' came out in spring 2006, followed by a second edition in spring 2007. *Elle* magazine came out with their first 'Green Issue' in May 2006, advising readers to: 'Clean up your act with Eco Chic Fashion, Travel, Food and Robert F. Kennedy Jr'. They followed up with a second 'Green Issue' in May 2007, with the strapline 'Eco Chic Heats Up'.

Tatler, Grazia, Harper, Red and *Women's Wear Daily* have all featured news items on green fashion. *Eve* magazine even went so far as to hire their first green correspondent, and *Harper's Bazaar*'s deputy editor, Harriet Green, has covered green fashion issues.

High fashion – from endorsement to influence

'The day that a big brand endorses eco-principles and makes it a selling point will be a prized moment for planet fashion and planet Earth,' the doyenne of the fashion press, Suzy Menkes, wrote in the *International Herald Tribune* in April 2006.

Just over one year later, in June 2007, Suzy Menkes headlined a story on Italy's Pitti Immagine Uomo fair: 'Green is good – by customer demand'. She stated that 'the burgeoning demand from a concerned public is creating a change in the fashion climate'. Ermenegildo Zegna had reportedly created a solar jacket that could recharge electronic gadgets using nature's energy, as well as a collection of leather accessories using non-chemical production. She said the long-term focus of the family is 'green, clean and environmentally friendly'. So was this the prized day for planet fashion and planet Earth?

Adding value and reducing risk in the business of fashion

The question that industry is asking is this: does it pay to be ethical? A sustainable business does not mean one that values environmental or social issues above profits – instead it means one which combines business strategies that meet its financial realities with measures aimed at protecting, sustaining and enhancing the human and natural resources needed in the future.

Adding value

Consultants A.T. Kearney's January 2007 survey of 25 companies found that CEOs believe sustainability is a 'top line' opportunity. In terms of adding value, it presents two opportunities. First, sustainability can be a revenue driver in the areas of product differentiation and increased demand, as consumers increasingly search out ethical clothes. Secondly, in the area of intangibles, sustainability can build brands and communities and improve employee morale.

To an increasing number of business leaders CSR policies are seen as necessary if a company is to compete successfully. A recent report released by Goldman Sachs, one of the world's leading investment banks, showed that companies that are considered leaders in implementing environmental, social and governance (ESG) policies to create sustained competitive advantage, have outperformed the general stock market by 25 per cent since August 2005. Of those companies, 72 per cent have outperformed their peers over the same period.[2]

Reducing negatives

The costs of doing nothing, on the other hand, can be high. Specifically, companies that don't implement sustainability measures have higher waste-disposal costs, higher energy and fuel costs, and higher input costs (for example packaging, chemicals, water).

Being sustainable also means reducing risk, as regards protecting a company's brand value and managing investor concerns. In addition, the potential liability of a sustainable company is likely to be lower than if it was not sustainable.

Mark Robertson, a spokesman for Ethical Investment Research Services (Eiris), says that 'ethical issues are now part of a company's general risk assessment', pushing them higher up the corporate agenda. 'As well as the risk to a firm's reputation, managing these issues badly can show poor governance. We find that companies which tackle these issues best tend to be the best managed.'

It is worth mentioning that another consultancy, Innovest Strategic Value Advisors, came to similar conclusions. Innovest is an international consultancy researching environmental, social and corporate governance issues on behalf of institutional investors. They found that companies which fall behind in ESG issues could underperform their peers financially. This is because the way a company handles political, environmental, labour and human rights risks is a powerful proxy and leading indicator of overall management quality.

These issues involve companies right down through the supply chain. The percentage of companies that have deselected suppliers for failing to meet sustainability criteria rose from only 17 per cent in 2002 to 60 per cent in 2007. Analysts A.T. Kearney predict that this will increase to 70 per cent in the future. This means that not only for retailers, but also for the suppliers they use, being 'green and ethical' will no longer be an option, it will be a necessity.

RITE on retailing

Reducing the Impact of Textiles on the Environment (RITE) Group was created by Marks & Spencer, University of Leeds and *Ecotextile News* as a new industry association aiming to provide advice and fact-based information to minimize the negative environmental impact of the production, use and disposal of textiles and apparel. RITE's ultimate goal is to drive forward the sustainable and ethical production of textiles and clothing throughout the global supply chain by means of a number of innovative initiatives. Its first conference was held in London in October 2007. Further details are available from their website: *www.ritegroup.org*.

A green department store? Barneys New York

'I do not think the eco/organic/fair-trade movement is a trend. I think it is the beginning of a major shift in consciousness in the fashion business.'

Julie Gilhart, fashion director and senior vice-president of Barneys New York

According to Julie Gilhart: 'It is very important that designers look for opportunities to support underprivileged communities. At any level of fashion, high or low, it doesn't matter ... Eco, green, organic, sustainable – there's no question it's a trend. It's the one trend you can't get enough of.'[3] Julie isn't just waxing lyrical about eco issues: she has introduced Barney's, one of the most 'directional' department stores in the fashion world, to green fashion. Organic brand Loomstate has created a 'Loomstate for Barneys Green' range. It was launched in March 2007, offering outerwear, organic-cotton and free-range alpaca sweaters, eco jeans in unwashed 100 per cent vegetable-dyed cotton. Barneys and Loomstate also donate a percentage of their sales to the 'One Percent for the Planet' environmental organization. Barneys are promoting green issues throughout the company through their 'eco' seminars in all stores and through written information sent out to sales associates.

Around the world in eco fashion: the 'Greening' of Fashion Weeks

London Fashion Week – Estethica

Estethica, an ethical space within the Designers Exhibition at London Fashion Week, is entirely devoted to the best in eco-sustainable high fashion. Co-curated with label From Somewhere (profiled in Chapter 8), Estethica 'offers the perfect opportunity for eco-friendly designers to gain mainstream exposure and to be associated with one of the most directional trade fairs in the world', according to Hilary Riva, chief executive of the British Fashion Council.

At its debut in September 2006, Estethica started off with 12 ethical and eco labels. It grew to 22 in February 2007 and 28 in September 2007. Hilary Riva says, 'Estethica is most definitely an important part of the Exhibition at London Fashion Week. The high-calibre designers who exhibit within Estethica bring a strong commercial and creative contribution to British fashion.'

Indeed, the fact that the British Fashion Council have officially sanctioned such a platform within London Fashion

Week is evidence that they are achieving their aims 'to position ethical labels within a mainstream fashion context and to raise awareness to an area which for many years has potentially been seen as a niche market'. Hilary Riva says, 'Trade as a whole is becoming more and more aware of ethical and sustainable production and is recognizing fair trade, organic production and recycling as important working methods.' Further information is available from their website: *www.estethica.com.*

Paris Prêt à Porter – So Ethic

February 2006 saw the first 'Autre Monde, Autre Mode' fashion exhibition at Paris's Prêt à Porter fair, which included 18 eco and ethical labels from around the world, primarily British and French. The Fédération Française du Prêt à Porter Feminin, or French Federation of Women's Ready-to-Wear, had been following the rise 'in official reports, the fashion media, and we had become aware of the fact that this was a rising movement,' says Matthew Allen, the brains behind the project.

After the first season, 'Autre Monde, Autre Mode' was renamed So Ethic, and it has continued to grow and grow – from 100 square metres of exhibition space to 600 square metres, and from 43 exhibitors at the fair in September 2006 to over 70 in February 2007 and more than 80 in September 2007.

Exhibitors have to conform to certain standards in one of three areas: social (fair labour practices), environmental (eco and recycled fabrics) and economic (reinvesting profits into communities).

The 'ethics' of So Ethic have begun to permeate the Prêt à Porter show and green issues have taken on a wider resonance. 'We are no longer printing catalogues – they will be sent to the press electronically, and at the February 2008 fair catalogues will be given out as memory sticks that you can use on personal computers,' says Matthew Allen. Not only are they reducing their printing, the 130 hosts and hostesses at the fair are all dressed in fair-trade organic T-shirts designed by Katharine Hamnett, and decked out in Terra Plana's vegetable-tanned eco shoes. Their 'thousands of metres' of carpeting will be recycled.

Around the same time as Paris fashion week, but not officially part of it, is the Ethical Fashion Show (EFS), a trade show open to the public and more like a market. Founded by Isabelle Quehe, the Ethical Fashion Show has a showroom and runway featuring eco-textile and community-centred fashion projects based in poor countries.

Berlin Premium Show – Green Area

For their very first ethical space, in July 2007 the 10th Premium dedicated a special area, the 'Green Area', to collections and brands that have embraced ethical and eco themes. Their annual symposium, which brings together 'luminaries from the international fashion industry – designers, product managers, buyers and representatives of the press', also discussed the theme 'Fashion and Ethics'.

New York Fashion Week – Edun

Edun, the ethical brand run by Bono and his wife, Ali Hewson, showed their collection at a catwalk show 'with a difference'. Instead of models, the group Citizens Band, and actors Zooey Deschanel and Rain Phoenix wore Edun's designs and performed songs about climate change and war.

Not part of NY fashion week, but around the same time, there is Limited Edition New York (L.E.N.Y). Mariel Gamboa, founder of the Paris trade show Tranoi, came up with Limited Edition New York under the motto 'Design for a cause and save the planet'. This project aims to mobilize the fashion industry in aid of Al Gore's Climate Project, to which 10 per cent of proceeds are donated.

For the first event, in September 2006, designers sold 'Save the Earth' themed wear – including a Diane von Furstenberg wrap dress with the words 'love the planet', items made with minimal harm to the environment (cashmeres, wools, linens and silks that used no chemical dyes), and limited-edition T-shirts created by Gwyneth Paltrow, Christy Turlington and Kate Moss.

The second event in September 2007 brought together designs from 30 brands – and included designers such as Calvin Klein and Lapo Elkann, who each created a one-of-a-kind piece around a common theme, and 20 'fashion icons' (Jade Jagger, Richard Branson), who designed an exclusive T-shirt or tote bag made of organic cotton. These were all shown in a gallery-like exhibition in New York's Industria Studio. Further information is available from the website *www.leny-icons.com.*

Sao Paulo – E Fabrics

During Sao Paulo fashion week in January 2007, there was an E Fabrics exhibition including 12 dresses all made from environmentally friendly alternative fabrics ranging from organic cotton to recycled PET to fish leather. The exhibition was the brainchild of designer Oscar Metzevat – of famous Brazilian brand Osklen. The exhibited dresses were made by famous Brazilian designers – asked to do so by Oscar. All the dresses came with an environmental fact sheet; the Paper dress, for example, revealed that 1 tonne of recycled paper promotes a saving of 10,000 litres of water and avoids the destruction of 17 mature trees.

Milan – White

White, the women's prêt-à-porter fashion show launched a platform to showcase sustainable eco-textiles and labels at their

September 2007 show. Slow White, an eco fashion exhibition highlighting around 12 brands will exhibit alongside Creative Lifestyle and Sustainable Synergies, or C.L.A.S.S, which highlights textile brands focusing on organic, chemical free and corn-based fabrics.

Design schools go eco[4]

Many of the country's leading design schools have recently incorporated sustainability issues into their curricula. Leading lights include:

Central St Martin's

As well as the course 'The Responsibilities of Consumption – Beyond Shopping', Central St Martin's BA (Hons) Fashion curriculum has a Sustainability Project in Year 2. This incorporates discussion around issues such as the human cost of fast fashion, labour standards, corporate social responsibility and what it means to workers, what kind of pressures can be exerted by business, codes of conduct, including human rights, waste treatment, monitoring of CSR and development of standards, the kinds of decisions routinely made by designers that can have impact on ethical standards, sustainable design including eco and recycled fabrics. Central St Martin's say that many students endeavour to incorporate an ethical or environmental element into their projects and final collections.

Chelsea School of Art

Chelsea's BA in Textile Design comprehensively covers a range of eco-textiles issues. All students are introduced to eco-textiles issues in the first year through theory and studio programmes. In the spring term they produce recycled garments for the

Alternative Fashion Show in Spitalfields, London. In the summer term they have a 'Green Textiles' lecture series.

The theory programme for Year 2 students in spring 2007 was called 'Contemporary Practice' and the visiting speakers were all designers who are currently exploring eco issues. The summer design project in 2007 was 'Short/Long Life Design', which resulted in a catwalk show in London.

By the third year, students can choose to write their final dissertation on eco-textile issues, and are encouraged to integrate this into their final graduate collection.

This eco-textile coursework is supported by the Textile Environment Design (TED) project and resource, which the students access from their first year onwards. Students are encouraged to be involved in this activity through internships and placements. The TED Materials Resource is an open-access facility that houses a collection of fabric samples, press cuttings, academic papers, dissertations, research projects and case studies.

London College of Fashion

In the summer of 2007, London College of Fashion (LCF) initiated a 'Green is the New Black' week of activities including staff development, workshops with students and local schools, film showings and a debate. The exhibition 'Green is the New Black' showcased ethical and sustainable fashion products and their unique journeys. A series of events is being planned for the next academic year.

LCF are also in the process of putting together a new MA in 'Fashion and the Environment'. They already have an ethical fashion elective open to second-year BA students, which explores issues around design or management following ethically and environmentally sound principles.

The curricula for many of the courses at undergraduate and

postgraduate level have incorporated issues relating to the responsibility of consumers to those involved in making products, and to the world. Fashion product courses include objectives relating to economically sound and sustainable practices. Projects include Re-think, Re-design, Remake.

Nottingham Trent University

Nottingham Trent University offer a 20-credit elective in ethical fashion. In the 2006 academic year, level 2 students worked on a live project with the Co-op promoting their fair-trade policies through fashion.

De Montfort University (Leicester)

De Montfort's BSc in Retail Buying includes research for two mini presentations covering ethical issues. The first investigates brands that were criticized for their trading polices and discusses how companies now are taking steps to ensure that workers are not being exploited to produce their products.

The second presentation is based on researching clothing brands that promote themselves as being either environmentally sensitive or are based on ethical trading. Students choose a brand and consider their policies and how successful they believe the company is in their approach. Are the retailers genuinely providing a more ethical/environmentally sound approach to business? Or does it just provide good PR and a point of differentiation? Students also consider how can brands criticized for their policies learn from these brands and what might be the benefits and the problems associated with adopting such an approach.

Finally, students consider how consumers can be influenced to encourage them to consider the ethics behind the label.

Chapter 6

Fabrics of the future

Fabrics today are being judged in a new light. While still essential, no longer is it sufficient just to wash and wear well, and whether or not they are sustainable is a mark of their quality. What is their overall environmental footprint and, through their manufacture, has any harm come to either humans or wildlife? Fabrics of the 21st century will have to compete on these new criteria.

Organic cotton fits the bill, as do a number of textiles that could be used to revive the ailing UK textile market – such as organic wool, organic leather and hemp. And as for synthetics, there is a range of alternatives that could take a bite out of the polyester giant. This chapter covers the whole gamut of these sustainable fabrics – as well as eco dyes, organic printing and the certification standards and labels to look out for when buying organic clothes.

Cleaning up cotton

Wander through the Victoria and Albert Museum's costume section and you get a glimpse of some of the most elaborate and remarkable clothes in the world. What's most shocking is that these centuries-old fabrics are actually all organic.

Until relatively recently our clothes were made from cotton that was grown organically. The growth of synthetic pesticides and fertilizers happened very quickly, corresponding to a population and technology boom, and cotton shot up to become the world's largest non-food crop. As a result, we are hard-pressed today to find cotton that hasn't been touched by the hand of modern chemistry.

Yet, looked at another way, in 2006 world demand for organic cotton exceeded supply for the first time. According to the Soil Association, the market for organic textiles in the UK is growing at 50 per cent per year, almost double that for the organic food market, at 26 per cent. While in practice organic cotton makes up only 0.19 per cent of the 25.5 million tonnes of cotton produced globally, there are clear indications and much optimism that organic cotton is being brought into the mainstream.[1]

Why organic cotton?

Contrary to conventional agriculture, the vast majority of organic cotton projects are set up directly to combat poverty, with social and economic goals an integral part of their make-up, according to Simon Ferrigno, director of the Farm Development Programme at Organic Exchange.[2]

Simon works with farm groups around the world, giving technical and business advice and has first-hand knowledge of the benefits that organic cotton growing can bring to the mainly small, often resource-poor farmers involved. There are currently 100,000 farming households involved in organic cotton, the majority of which are in India and Africa. This number is set to grow because major benefits of organic farming include:

Increased income and better health for cotton farmers

Organic Exchange surveyed seven groups of farmers in India on their experiences before and after organic farming and found that six farm groups reported much higher incomes and similar or higher yields per hectare. The seventh farm group reported the same level of income as with conventional cotton, but with lower health costs from reduced exposure to pesticides.[3] Indeed, farmers' exposure to toxic pesticides is reduced or eliminated by switching to organics.

Premiums paid for organic cotton

Farmers usually receive a 20 per cent premium for organic cotton, which may rise in the future as a full impact model, calculating the total costs of producing organic cotton, is worked out.

Better long-term yields

In the long term, yields for organic cotton outperform those for conventional cotton. In the short term, two–three years, there are losses as the health of the soil is slowly restored. 'But in the five-to-seven-year period, as a whole, organic cotton fares much better than cotton. This is most notably the case in countries such as Uganda, Tanzania and Paraguay,' according to Simon Ferrigno.

Farmers and communities have more say

Co-operatives and farmer-owned initiatives have proved to be the most successful organic cotton projects. With most conventional cotton, farmers aren't an active part of the supply chain, as they sell to a trader offering them a fixed price. With organic-cotton farming groups, farmers have a stake in the process and have more choice over their buyers. Organic-cotton farming groups also benefit communities – such as in Koussanar, Senegal, where farmers have organized themselves into village unions and are working together to branch out into other crops such as rice and vegetables (ensuring better food security) while developing a local textile manufacturing base.

Better for the soil and the environment

As regards the environment, organic cotton is a major improvement to conventional cotton in terms of protecting local wildlife and the health of the soil. Soil on organic farms is more able to sustain life – in essence, having healthier soil is like having a healthier immune system. Organic cotton farms are more adaptable to climate change and survive better in extreme weather conditions, which will become more important as the impacts of climate change increase. As LaRhea Pepper, a US-based organic cotton farmer, put it, 'Farmers are on a chemical treadmill. They say, "This year my soil needs this much synthetic, petroleum-based fertilizer to make this grow. Next year it will need more." What you have is soil that is nothing less than a drug addict.'

Organic cotton in figures[4]

- Global retail sales of organic cotton products increased from $245 million (£118.7 million) in 2001 to $583 (£282.6 million) in 2005, reflecting an average annual growth rate of 35 per cent.

- The number of small brands and retailers in North American, European and Asian markets had mushroomed from a few hundred to more than 1,200 companies by the end of 2005.

- Global organic product sales are projected to skyrocket to $2.6 billion (£1.26 billion) by the end of 2008, reflecting an average annual growth rate of 116 per cent.

What needs to happen now

In 2006, for the first time ever, demand for organic cotton exceeded supply. In order for production to grow fast enough to meet demand, key issues need to be addressed. These include:

Finance

Many organic cotton projects are funded as part of EU governments' development aid. While this type of support is useful in the conversion process, it acts as a type of subsidy and may ultimately create an unfair market. Investment is needed from players who will ultimately not only help support the farmers but assure them there is a market for their goods at the end of it. Big retailers, such as Tesco and Marks & Spencer, have expressed interest in supporting farmers to make the transition from conventional to organic cotton, as well as the Taiwanese government and certain UN bodies. Whether through direct finance, loans or other means, support from these institutions would, at the very least, enable farmers to approach local lending agencies with the confidence that they would be able to repay them.

Planning

Because the market is still in its embryonic stages, brands and retailers need to incorporate organic cotton into long-term planning. Making commitments will help farmers plan ahead. As organic cotton farmer LaRhea Pepper says, 'You can't just push a button and make a pink shirt appear. What's in a store today will have been planned by most companies a couple years ago and farmers will have planted it three years ago.'

Support networks, training and research

Conventional farmers have the benefit of long-established networks, in the form of research centres, information and advice. Organic cotton farmers have little or no opportunity to fall back on these support networks. One thing that is often not recognized is that farmers are constantly learning – which species of cotton is most suitable for different climates, for example, and what are the new and pioneering farming techniques being created. ·

'There are very good training centres in Zambia and Paraguay and in Benin, but overall it's patchy,' according to Simon Ferrigno. That will change as governments in Africa continue to support university programmes. Uganda has by far the most extensive farmer support and training system, and the government has been instrumental in making this happen. (Bono's label Edun source their Live T-shirts from Uganda.) Other governments are considering this model.

Certification

Organic certification has already been established, but in order for the pool of organic farmers to increase a separate certification scheme may be developed to recognize 'organic cotton in conversion' on a global level. Plans to develop such a certification scheme are in very early stages and may involve the UN body UNCTAD (United Nations Conference on Trade and Development). A 'cotton in conversion' standard would go a long way to recognizing farmers who have started on the path to organics and enable them to recoup part of the costs of conversion.

Certification can be expensive. Some developing countries or regions have their own certification, notably India and Uganda. But most times, farmers need to be accredited by European or North American standards, which can be prohibitively expensive. Developing own-country or region standards would lower costs.

Organic cotton retailers

Jan Schriver, partner of pioneer organic cotton company
Bo Weevil, works with local NGOs (non-governmental
organizations) in developing nations to support organic cotton
farmers, including the renowned Lango project in Uganda. Bo
Weevil's Ecotton collections offer T-shirts and leisurewear for
men, women and children, as well as home accessories.

Green Fibres, founded by William and Gaby Lana, have been
instrumental in developing certification standards for organic
cotton textiles, and through their website they sell a wide
range of undyed, unbleached organic cotton basics and
home accessories.

Gossypium (the botanical name for cotton) is a brand created
in India in 1998 to open the market for 'cottons that would be
environmentally and socially positive for the grower and his
capital – the soil,' says co-founder Abigail Petit. Their cotton-
trading partner, Agrocel, is a shareholder in the Gossypium
brand, 'which ensures that the cotton farmers will always have a
voice on our board,' she says. Gossypium offer slogan T-shirts
and men's and women's basics, as well as bed and bath linen.

Converting company execs
to organic cotton

The California-based Sustainable Cotton Project leads annual
farm tours to introduce clothing company executives to cotton
farmers who are reducing their chemical use. Over the past ten

years, this has influenced many companies that may not have otherwise contemplated it, to consider using organic cotton. Such companies include Esprit, Patagonia, Nike, Marks & Spencer, IKEA, Eileen Fisher and Levi.[5]

Several major US brands use a small proportion of organic cotton in some of their garments. These include Nike and Timberland. Other retailers that have made long-term commitments to organic cotton include Marks & Spencer, Wal-Mart and Woolworths.

The future of 'Made in the UK': organic wool, leather and hemp

The textile industry in the UK has been declining for decades, and it still is. Organic farming in the UK is on the rise, but at the moment the wool from organically reared sheep and the hides of organically reared cows are not valued as such. Creating networks to separate and process these fabrics, as well as the development of a new 'wonder crop', hemp, could go a long way to bringing on a revival of 'Made in the UK' clothes. The knock-on effects from this would be many: reducing 'clothes miles' is sure to be a subject of much concern in coming years; supporting marginalized communities in our own backyard; safeguarding communities, the countryside and traditional skills; and proving that fair trade begins at home.

Reviving the countryside – organic wool

Organic wool may be one of the answers to how to revive the seemingly terminally-ill wool market. There are currently 4,000 certified organic farms in the UK. The number of organically reared sheep on these farms was 691,000 at the last count. If processed in an organic supply chain, this would result in 691,000 kilograms of premium organic wool fabric.

The reality today is that the majority of UK wool – organic or not – goes to making carpeting. Because of the extremely low price that farmers get for wool in the UK and the unsuitability of sheep breeds used, the UK wool market has been on the decline for decades.

One of the most popular breeds in the UK is the Blackface Sheep, the wool from which, because it is so coarse and thick, is never good for clothes, but is valuable for making carpets and mattressing. There is a historical reason for this: when the price of wool was agreed farmers were encouraged to specialize in sheep with more wool, so other breeds, which produced less wool, suffered.

Organic farmers are more imaginative regarding the sheep they breed, opting instead for breeds such as Hebridean, Cheviot or Lleyn. These are less common breeds that thrive in lowlands and produce a finer wool fibre, which is more useful than coarse wool for spinners and weavers.

Isle of Mull Weavers is a pioneering initiative giving the wool from these rarer breeds of sheep a greater worth – all the while creating a sustainable way of life for small farmers and safeguarding age-old craftsmanship and traditions. They have combined textures and weaves to produce the country's first collection of organic tweed, including tailored sports coats and ladies' jackets as well as organic scarves, rugs and throws.

Isle of Mull Weavers was founded by Bob and Cathy Ryan in 1987. Bob, a lifetime weaver, switched his farm to native Hebridean breeds from the commercial Blackface and decreased the number from 600 to 200 sheep. 'Hebrideans are a better breed for the land, the land has flourished, and we get a better income from the wool and by selling our meat ourselves,' says Aeneas Mackey, who has run the farm with his wife, Minty, for ten years. Eight years ago they converted to organic.

With their 200 Hebridean sheep, they produce 200 kilograms of wool. The rest of their 2.5 tonnes of wool comes from around the country – from such esoteric-sounding breeds as the Castlemilk Moorit, Manx Loghtan and from the Shetland Organic Producers Organization (SOPG), which includes ten farmers rearing native Shetland hill sheep. Almost two-thirds of the wool is organic, but it is not certified as organic because smaller farmers cannot afford the cost of organic certification.

'When we started weaving Hebridean wool, I was inundated with requests from breeders who didn't know what to do with their wool.' Aeneas estimates that there are between 2,000 and 3,000 registered Hebridean sheep in the UK, and another 3,000 unregistered. 'On the whole of the Isle of Mull, there are perhaps 20,000 sheep. If all of these were native Hebridean breeds, our entire weaving operation could be run from just farmers on the Isle of Mull.'

This is a long-term vision, but in the very short term Isle of Mull Weavers have created a market for wool that was once worthless. It cost farmers almost £1 a kilogram to clip a sheep and transport its wool, but a quick glance at the British Wool Marketing Board's website (they buy and sell the UK's wool) reveals that the average price per kilogram is only 72 pence. Isle of Mull Weavers currently pay £1.25 per kilogram for their wool. This is because Aeneas believes that fair trade begins at home.

The wool is spun by hand and woven using what Aeneas describes as 'a very dependable but ancient mechanical 1930s loom'. The products are unique as the colours of the yarn vary from sheep to sheep. The undyed brown and black fleece of the

Ardalanish Hebridean sheep is mixed with the natural whites and fawns of Shetland wool from the SOPG farmers.

'It's been difficult to make the whole process organic. Aside from the wool, there is organic scouring, organic spinning and organic finishing – which has been the most difficult,' says Aeneas. Soil Association standards for organic wool won't allow non-biodegradable detergents to be used or those with high aquatic toxicity; there is no bleaching; they put limits on heavy metals so environmentally friendly alternatives to chrome dyes are needed. Isle of Mull Weavers have had to rope in other smaller organizations – also certified organic – to perform parts of the manufacturing process. But the next stage is to develop their own scouring and spinning facilities.

This is a local cottage industry, but one that started from the bottom up. It has had clear benefits for the community. And while this may not represent a mass-market initiative, their products find a natural home in high-quality tailoring outfits such as in Savile Row, and other specialist markets.

Hemp on the high street

There is huge potential for hemp as a sustainable eco textile especially when compared to synthetics and non-organic cotton. People may sneer, but the THC (tetrahydrocannabinol), the active narcotic ingredient in the plant, is present in small enough quantities for hemp growing to have been made legal again in 1994.

Farmers looking to diversify took up the challenge, knowing that there was a market for hemp fibres for interiors and in the car industry. In the UK, hemp has been grown on around 2,000 hectares every year since the early nineties. But it is mainly to produce animal bedding, cigarette paper pulp, fibre and recyclable car interiors.

Hemp as a textile fabric has much potential. It 'breathes' and so keeps you cool in hot weather, and is soft, comfortable and yet hard-wearing. And as a crop the benefits are well known. Hemp is considered a miracle plant: it has a very cleansing effect on the land; it adds nutrients so is an ideal 'break' crop, to be grown in between other crops; it grows as a very thick canopy, suppressing weeds, so it is more naturally 'organic'. In essence, it is a very low input crop, reducing the need to use artificial pesticides and fertilizers.

Currently in the UK, there is no factory or mill with experience of spinning, weaving or knitting hemp. The hemp clothing found in the UK is produced in China and Eastern Europe.

BioRegional Development Group, an independent environmental organization that develop commercially viable products and services, have attempted to revive the UK textile market by starting a research project with Hemcore, the UK's largest hemp growing organization. The project involves 1,214 hectares of hemp fields grown by 50 different farmers under contract, mainly in south-east England. BioRegional, along with Hemcore and help from the University of Leeds, and with funding from what was formerly the Department of Trade and Industry, have done hemp harvesting trials and are looking at new, more environmentally friendly processing methods.

'If we can find a way to extract the fibres, there should be no problem creating a market. We want to see hemp on the high street,' says project director Emily Stott. They are developing a technology to produce a fine enough fibre to be spun in traditional, but almost defunct, UK cotton mills, including one in Huddersfield. Hemp could also be spun using the wool spinning system, but the project team are finding it difficult to gain support for this, as there is an issue of contaminating the spinning mill with hemp fibres.

If it can be spun and woven in the UK, there would be increased commercial potential for hemp as a mainstream clothing fabric.

Eco leather

At least 90 per cent of the leather worldwide is chrome tanned. Vegetable tanning, while thousands of years old, contributes only a very small percentage of tanned leather. It is an ancient process whereby, in essentially a single step, the extract of tree bark or vegetables is absorbed into the material. Traditional vegetable tanning produces leather that can be stiff, and is successfully used for horse saddles, harnesses and boots for the Queen's guard, but current-generation veg-tanned leather is supple and soft.

Totnes-based Green Shoes produce vegetable-tanned leather shoes. For the last 25 years, Alison Hastie has been making bespoke leather shoes in her workshop, originally using leather cast-offs from Clarks shoes, based in Somerset. Green Shoes' veg-tanned leather uses natural plant leaves and seed pods – these vegetable and plant oils condition the tanned hides, so the leather is gorgeous and soft. It is free from heavy metals and toxins, so is kind to your skin. Veg-tanned leather also makes for a more individual product as each hide has variations in colour and tone. Green Shoes produce bark, berry and natural ebony veg-tanned leathers.

There is another means of obtaining 'green' leather, which is to use certified organic leather. There is only one licensee in the UK: ROMP, run by Greg Sturmer. They source their leather from UK organic farms and tan it in a Slovenian tannery, Industrija usnja Vrhnika (IUV). According to Lee Holdstock of the Soil Association, 'Unless you have someone like Greg specifically sourcing leather hides from organically reared cows, organic farmers' hides go to hide merchants, who come and simply take their hides away, mixing them with the rest of the lot.' A lot of these go to China to be tanned. 'We are so into the idea of devolution, but why not have county constabularies with leather equipment that comes from organic leather from their own county,' he adds.

The Soil Association have certification standards for 'organic leather', which, apart from coming from organically reared cows, is tanned organically. In essence, this means it is vegetable tanned with restrictions on inputs from other processes, including hide pickling and dehairing.

Yet another sustainable leather alternative is recycled leather. The traditional leather-cutting process is hugely wasteful. The shape of the leather hide, as we know, is irregular, so it is trimmed to give it a uniform shape, and to give a uniform thickness only the top layer is shaved off and used. The offcuts are simply considered waste. But this trimming waste can be from 18 to as much as 40 per cent of a hide.

E-Leather is a Peterborough-based company that takes leather waste and creates a 'sandwich product': the two outer layers are of leather fibre and through the middle is a textile core, which, currently, is usually polyester or nylon but can be cotton. According to sales manager Andrew Hudson, polyester is needed to add to the strength. Because E-Leather is supplied in uniform rolls, it drastically reduces the cutting waste to 5 per cent. E-Leather is used by shoemakers Terra Plana and there is a possibility it will be used by Marks & Spencer.

The idea started in 1995, when inventor Chris Bevan, now E-Leather chairman, won a Department of Trade and Industry Smart Award to investigate technology. Twelve years and $30 million (£14.5 million) later, through a series of government funding and private investors, they have taken it to the stage where they now have a 9,000 square metre high-tech factory capable of processing 2 million square metres of their product per year. This equates to saving 2,400 tonnes of leather waste a year from going to landfill. E-Leather have been running since November 2006.

Most of their leather is from the UK. Their suppliers get a cost saving, as it usually costs £500 per tonne to dispose of their leather waste. E-Leather processing has also made great strides in clean manufacturing – there are no water drains on site, waste water is recycled, no acids or salts are used, and dyes are water based.

The future of synthetics?

Replacing synthetics with renewable raw materials to make 'compostable synthetics' is the way forward to sustainability.

• Ingeo – Pegging itself as 'the world's first 100 per cent man-made fibre from annually renewable sources', Ingeo is being heralded in the US as the new miracle fibre and beginning to be noticed in Europe as well. Made from corn, it is processed to release sugars that are fermented to produce a biodegradable thermoplastic, Polylactide (PLA). PLA can also be produced from sugar cane. Just like other man-made fibres, it is then melted and extruded to produce the fibre. Ingeo, a brand name marketed by Cargill Dow, one of the world's biggest food companies, can have the texture of fine cotton and possesses superior moisture-management properties. Once only considered for use in sportswear fabrics, PLA garments have been made by Armani, Diesel and Dutch designer Rianne de Witte. PLA can be composted, not in your back garden, but in industrial facilities. Contention about the fabric arises over the issue of genetically modified (GM) corn. The corn for Ingeo comes from producers in the US's 'corn belt' in the mid-west, of which a high percentage is GM. This is something that Cargill will have to address because many consumers are opposed to GM products, especially in a garment marketed as sustainable. For others, compared to petroleum-based synthetic fabrics, GM is the lesser of two evils.

* Eco rayon and viscose – Hardly a new kid on the block, Austrian-based Lenzig Group produce around 450,000 tonnes of fibre per year, and have over 40 years' experience making fabrics with sustainable materials. They make cellulosic fibres based mainly on wood, including sustainably managed (Forest Stewardship Council certified) beech to make Modal, and eucalyptus trees to make Tencel. Modal is touted as a luxury fabric for lingerie, sleepwear and leisurewear as it has softness next to the skin. Tencel, according to Lenzig, 'is as fine as silk, as strong as polyester, as easy to care for as acrylic, cool and pleasant like linen, as warm as wool and absorbs more moisture than cotton'. It can be used as denim, woven fabrics and knitwear. They both, like PLA, are compostable. The Lenzig factory uses a closed-loop system, ensuring the pulping process is low impact and waste water is of drinking quality.

* Bamboo, soya, banana leaves and milk starch – These are other sustainable materials being experimented with as fabrics.

Vegan fabrics

• Vegan leathers – While some in the eco fashion movement believe the argument that replacing animal hides with non-biodegradable plastics doesn't hold, 'cruelty-free leathers' have allowed vegans and vegetarians to expand their wardrobes while sticking to their beliefs. Nathalie Dean is one of these. She became a vegan in 2000 and it 'opened a can of worms' in terms of forcing her to look at aspects of her lifestyle that were affected. The problem was, as she says, that she 'lived in stilettos'. With no shoe background, but with a belief in merging ethics and fashion, she started trading in 2003 under the name of Beyond Skin, producing handmade women's shoes using fabrics such as organic denim, hemp, faux leathers and suedes, satins and heavy cottons. Her vegan leathers are all polyurethane (PU), which is 'much gentler on the environment than PVC', she says. She uses a small manufacturer in east London. Beyond Skin have a wide range of women's heels, flats and pumps and, as their website says, they are worn by Heather Mills and Natalie Portman. Others in the fashionably vegan leather camp include US-based Charmoné shoes, which use high-quality Italian microfibres, structured exactly like leather and therefore breathable, lightweight and colour-fast, to make women's fashion shoes. Canadian-based Matt & Nat produce a 'fashion-forward line of vegan handbags' as well as wallets and other accessories in a range of styles and colours. They use PU as well as polyvinyl chloride (PVC).

• Alternative Silk – From eco, organic and vegetarian silk to 'live silk' and even 'peace silk' – all are essentially a way of producing this luxury fabric in an alternative non-violent way. The most common procedure for silk making is by killing silk moths in their pupae stage, usually by boiling them alive within their cocoons. A more humane way of producing silk has now been invented – a method that allows the silkworms to live their full life cycle and also produce the fabric. This method encourages silkworms to spin the thread directly into sheets forming the fabric. Used in India and by UK-based producers such as Sally Barton.

Eco dyes

Can dyes ever really be all-natural? Can eco dyes ever be commercially viable? These are the questions that many in the industry – from artisanal natural dyers through to big multi-national dyeing companies – are beginning to ask.

While natural dyeing can be done on an industrial scale, traditionally dyes were applied by trained craftsmen. One of the UK's few natural dyers, Gracie Burnett, designs and dyes her clothing collection using entirely natural dyes. She has a colour garden where she grows the traditional UK plant dyestuffs: woad (the UK version of indigo that makes blue); madder (the root of a plant used to produce ochre and red); and weld, used to produce yellow dye. Another natural dye, cochineal, derived from beetles that die when they mate, is used to produce pink or purple. 'Mixing these four natural dyestuffs, you can create all the colours of the rainbow, with the exception of electric blues and fluorescent colours,' she says.

While there is no push, as yet, to natural dye on a large commercial scale, natural dyeing is gaining mainstream significance through the creation of 'eco jeans'. 'One of the most beautiful things to watch is the indigo dyeing process. When the cloth goes into an indigo vat, it comes out yellow. Only when it hits air does it turn the blue we know in typical blue jeans,' says Gracie. Synthetic indigo has to mimic this chemical reaction with synthetic dyes.

But natural dyes are not without controversy. According to some, there is a fallacy about eco dyes because mordants are needed to fix the dyes to the fabric; these generally include heavy metals. 'The colours aren't always as bright and strong, they are not as colour-fast as we're used to and are colouristically weak – lots of beet or natural resources are needed to make the colour,' says Peter Johnson of Huntsman, one of the biggest synthetic dye companies, based in Switzerland. Huntsman, instead, have developed several ranges of dyes suitable for use on an organically certified garment. 'For cotton, wool and silk, there are over 100 dyes where we have eliminated AOX, amines, banned carcinogenic heavy metals, except for some copper needed for bright yellows. They are generally free of formaldehyde, with no finishing agents other than softeners.'

But in the sustainability debate, natural dyes are one up on synthetic dyes. They are inherently biodegradable and carbon neutral. According to Gracie Burnett, 'Any big company is going to say natural dyeing is rubbish. But for example, indigo doesn't need a mordant. The only mordant I use is alum, a mineral salt, which is almost completely absorbed in the cloth, so the water is fine. Natural dyeing is expensive and physically hard work, if done all manually as I do it.'

Naturally coloured cotton

Naturally coloured cotton is available in shades of green, beige, brown and blue, some with a fibre length long enough to mill. Naturally coloured cotton cuts out the bleaching and dyeing process. Sally Fox's FoxFibre and UK-based Pakucho sell naturally coloured cotton that has been grown in South America and the south-west US.

Eco printing: T Shirt and Sons

In 2006, T Shirt and Sons, an established T-shirt printer with over 20 years of experience, was awarded the first licence for organic textile printing – the first and only in the UK.

Brothers John and Andy Lunt co-founded T Shirt and Sons in Bath in the 1980s. 'In many conventional printers, aromatic solvents are poured right down the drain,' says Andy. Solvents can harm the health and safety of workers as well as aquatic life. Fed up with this situation and 'because we believe in it', they started working with the Soil Association in 2003 to become organic. Overall it took three years, mainly because there were, and still are, no explicit rules for certifying organic printing. Instead they had to interpret organic rules for agriculture and other processes into their business practices and work out whether 'this would be sufficient'. In a trial and error process, they eventually covered their waste-management practices, the type of ink they use, and the ingredients in it (water-based ink that has eliminated the traditional formaldehyde, PVC, plastisols, phthalates).

All the T-shirts they produce, roughly half a million a year, are printed organically. 'It's not difficult but it is time-consuming,' says Andy. 'We've saved a lot of money going organic. We spend much less on waste management, for example.' T Shirt and Sons are used by Katharine Hamnett, Greenpeace and the Glastonbury Festival.

What is a 100 per cent organic garment?

In February 2003, the Soil Association launched standards covering the processing and manufacture of all natural fibres including leather and skins. This certification dictates what happens to organic cotton after it leaves the farm on its way to become a garment. If you are shopping in the UK, look out for Soil Association labels. Efforts to make these standards global led to major certifiers getting together to harmonize, resulting in the Global Organic Trading Standards (GOTS). The certifiers involved include the UK's Soil Association, Germany's NaturLand, the Institute of Market Ecology (IMO) in Switzerland, and Skal International, which has now become Control Unions in the Netherlands. So if you are outside the UK, look for GOTS – *www.global-standards.org.*

Standards include:

* All inputs must be assessed on their biodegradability and their toxicity to fish, algae and water fleas. In addition, inputs are not allowed if it is suspected, or proved, that the chemicals or processes used can cause cancer, birth defects or changes to reproductive organs. Suspected or proved allergens are also banned.

- A number of inputs are specifically prohibited including: fluorocarbons; halogenated flameproof agents; halogenated anti-moth agents; heavy metals (excluding iron); organochloride carriers and other chlorinated compounds; pyrethroids and chlorinated or perborate bleaching agents.

- Natural dyes from plants or insects that have been organically produced must be used where available in sufficient quality and quantity.

- GM products are not allowed.

- Over half of all dyes currently used contain 'AZO groups'. Made from a nitrogen bond, these give molecules their colour but, under reductive conditions, they can cleave to form amines. Some of these aromatic amines have been shown to be carcinogenic and 22 are effectively prohibited in the EU.

Other schemes to clean up clothes

- Ecocert is the certification used by French farmers and manufacturers and in French-speaking countries in Africa.

- The International Standards Organization's ISO 14001 standard reviews the environmental aspects of a company's products and services and outlines measures to reduce the environmental impact of processes from resource inputs to the final product and how it is disposed of.

- Oeko-tex Standard 100 scheme is run by the independent 'International Association for Research and Testing in the Field of Textile Ecology' and operated by franchized testing institutes in Europe, Asia and US. Over 6,000 companies worldwide have been awarded Oeko-Tex Standard 100 certification. Oeko-tex Standard 100 is concerned with possible negative effects of textiles on the health of the wearer. The latest version of the standard has four basic product categories: baby wear, textiles in contact with the skin, textiles not in contact with the skin and household textiles. It puts specific limits on harmful chemicals traditionally used in the manufacturing process.

Chapter 7

What's fair is fair labour

'Clearly fast fashion has a huge number of costs that we simply are not reckoning with.'

Safia Minney, founder of People Tree

Developing countries account for almost three-quarters of world clothing exports. So three out of every four garments sold in the West have come from a poor country. There are some 100 million garment workers worldwide who gin, spin, dye, cut, knit, weave, sew, trim, press, package and everything else involved in the clothes-making process. Many of them, as we know, are getting a raw deal. To add to that, there are perhaps millions more with traditional artisanal clothes-making skills, such as hand embroiderers, who are at the mercy of a globalized textile industry with innumerable market barriers. They work long hours, with few benefits, sometimes none, and for low pay. So what, if anything, can anyone do about it?

Founded in 1919, the International Labour Organization (ILO), an agency of the United Nations, exists to advance the 'decent treatment' of working people. It is the global body responsible for drawing up and overseeing international labour standards. ILO's core conventions cover the freedom of association (right to collective bargaining); the elimination of forced or compulsory labour; the abolition of child labour; and the elimination of discrimination at work. In principle, governments should adopt ILO conventions and incorporate them into national labour laws enforced by labour inspectors. Currently over 1,200 of these conventions have been ratified, representing 86 per cent of the possible number that could be ratified.

In practice, what happens in many countries is something different. ILO's protections have broken down because of the lack of either funds or the political will to enforce them. At the same time, big Western retailers which operate in developing countries need to protect their 'brand' image and, in a more altruistic way, are responsible for ensuring that the workers putting together their clothes are treated fairly. More and more often they are joining multi-stakeholder ethical trading initiatives (MSIs) – which involves signing up to a Code of Conduct based upon ILO conventions. Multi-stakeholder initiatives bring together retailers, trade unions, consumer groups, workers and sometimes governments.

Multi-stakeholder initiatives

It's easy to be cynical about MSIs as companies are not legally bound to abide by them. All the same, signing up to an MSI does show a level of commitment; it means that somewhere high up in the management there is an aim to source ethically. What all MSIs have in common is that they bring a wide range of actors into decision-making and design follow-up activities to put labour standards into effect.

Below are the top five internationally recognized MSIs and the verdict on how well they actually work.

Fair Labor Association (FLA)
www.fairlabor.org
This Washington DC-based initiative brings together major companies such as H&M, Liz Claiborne, Nike, Patagonia and Reebok, as well as 194 colleges and universities and NGOs. It began in 1996 after President Bill Clinton issued a challenge to apparel companies to do something about the constant revelations of sweatshop labour in the industry. Universities have long been core participants in FLA – in their attempts to stamp out sweatshop labour in the manufacturing process of products

bearing university logos. Members commit to upholding standards covering forced labour, child labour, abuse, discrimination, work environment, freedom of association, minimum wage and benefits, work-week hours and overtime pay.

Verdict: Communications director Alex Wohl says that companies do find it a challenge to apply their Code of Conduct, but adds, 'If there wasn't such a need, it probably wouldn't be a challenge.' FLA doesn't monitor or verify factories itself but does have a complaints mechanism. Through independent monitors, FLA has helped instigate more than 600 unannounced factory inspections in the last four years. Violations in any of their codes are publicly reported and flagged for immediate corrective action. For example, a monitor visiting a Chinese factory found that workers were not being paid. Member companies then required the factory to make back payments by the next pay period, and FLA helped companies ensure wage policies were created, implemented and communicated to workers.

Ethical Trading Initiative (ETI)

www.ethicaltrade.org

Now the UK's biggest multi-stakeholder initiative, ETI, established in 1998, represents 40 companies with a combined annual turnover of £107 billion. Retailer members include the Body Shop, Boots, Gap Inc., Marks & Spencer, Primark, Sainsbury's, Tesco and Zara. These companies are brought to the table with trade unions, development charities and campaigning organizations such as the TUC, the International Textile Garment and Leather Workers' Federation, Oxfam, Save the Children and Christian Aid.

All companies that join ETI are required to adopt the ETI

Base Code and the accompanying Principles of Implementation, which they must progressively introduce throughout their supply chain to ensure that they gradually improve workers' conditions. The aim is for continual improvement. They are required to submit a report to the ETI board every year, detailing their progress.

Verdict: ETI media relations manager Julia Hawkins says, 'One of the benefits of initiatives like ETI is that companies can talk openly, honestly among each other and with the trade unions and NGOs. For companies it offers a sense of not being alone in trying to effect change.' She says that ETI is aspirational: 'The principles are tricky to implement but there has to be a commitment to the principles.'

An ETI factsheet says that being a member of ETI 'does not necessarily mean that workers' rights are fully protected throughout their supply chain. It does mean that member companies have made serious commitments to improving conditions over time.'

Levi Strauss & Co were suspended and then resigned from ETI after refusing to adopt the Living Wage provision of the base code. Levi Strauss's position is that it cannot responsibly commit to the Living Wage provision because it does not believe it can implement it with its suppliers.

Primark joined ETI in 2006, and campaign group War on Want published a report the following December after interviewing workers at factories in Bangladesh that supply to ETI members Primark, Tesco and Asda. The report found that workers were typically paid 5p an hour and worked 80 hours a week. Clearly this was something ETI needed to step in and help remedy.

So is ETI a shield or does it result in improvement? According to Sam Maher of Labour Behind the Label, 'It depends on how you look at it. None of the companies can guarantee that all parts of their supply chain implement the ETI Base Code. The main issue is that there is no transparency – the reviews, criteria for inclusion and exclusion in ETI are all confidential, so as a pressure group it is hard to know what to try to hold them to. What is useful is that when there is an urgent issue involving a specific violation, it's much easier for us to get the companies involved to sit around a table and discuss the issue – we just ring up ETI and they ask the companies. Companies like Next are putting work in to improve practices.'

Fair Wear Foundation (FWF)
http://en.fairwear.nl/

Although based in the Netherlands, FWF has Europe-wide stakeholders – members include Mexx, O'Neil and Expresso Fashion, and campaign groups Oxfam and the Clean Clothes Campaign. Members accept the Code of Labour Practices then formulate a work plan for implementing it. All suppliers are informed of the code and are asked to subscribe to the labour standards, to co-operate with their gradual implementation, and to inform their employees about the labour standards, audits and future corrective action plans. During the first year of membership, a minimum of 40 per cent of the supply base must be audited; during the second year 60 per cent; and in the third year the entire supply base. Factory audits are repeated annually. The member company agrees on corrective action plans with its suppliers, and sees to it that they are carried out. Members must report annually on the progress they are making on implementing the code of labour practices.

Verdict: FWF verifies whether labour conditions are being met by means of unannounced visits to production companies, a complaints procedure for workers and others, and checking the books of member companies. Their main strength is their monitoring programmes – they train and build up local teams of auditors who have specific local knowledge and language skills, and can build up strong relationships with workers. FWF actively works with member companies to remedy any problems.

Worker Rights Consortium (WRC)
www.workersrights.org

A non-profit organization created by college and university administrations, students and labour rights experts in the US, WRC's purpose is to assist in the enforcement of manufacturing Codes of Conduct adopted by colleges and universities. These codes are designed to ensure that factories producing clothing and other goods bearing college and university names respect the basic rights of workers. There are more than 100 colleges and universities affiliated with WRC at present. WRC works with labour rights experts in the United States and around the world to investigate factory conditions.

Verdict: There is honest reporting of the complaints they receive, and the reports are available to the public from their website. A cynical view is that perhaps the reason why WRC is so refreshing is that they do not count companies among their members. They have monitoring systems to verify factories, using local monitors. WRC has 'one of the best-developed complaints-based systems, that starts to function when workers, or organizations representing workers, "pull the fire alarm",' according to the Clean Clothes Campaign.

Social Accountability International (SAI)

www.sa-intl.org

Founded in 1997, SAI is an accreditation and standards-setting organization. It can certify specific workplaces and factories. Social Accountability 8000 (SA8000) is a voluntary, universal standard for companies interested in auditing and certifying labour practices in their facilities and in those of their suppliers and vendors. There are currently 1,038 SA8000-certified facilities in 55 different countries and 58 different industries. Factory certification is based on complying with ILO conventions and other human rights standards.

Verdict: According to critics, SA8000 certification is based on minimum standards. Labour Behind the Label (LBL) have responded to labour rights violations at SA-certified factories. As Sam Maher from LBL says, 'It is not known how many, or if there are any factories that were audited but failed to achieve SA8000 certification.'

How can I tell if a garment is made in a sweatshop?

Unfortunately there are no easy answers. The sad truth is that even if a garment is relatively expensive it could still have been made in a sweatshop. According to Martin Hearson, campaign co-ordinator for Labour Behind the Label, 'The problems are structural and apply across the board, we need to engage the industry as a whole. The right question for people to ask is: "How can I persuade companies to do more to improve the conditions of workers on the ground?" It's not just about the particular pair of trousers you buy.'[1]

Before you buy, ask retailers three questions:

1 How much are the people producing the clothes you sell being paid? Some companies say that a 'living wage' for workers would not be possible and there is debate in the apparel industry about the process of calculating a living wage. Yet the Worker Rights Consortium argue that a calculated living wage for workers should cover the cost of meeting a family's basic needs in the following categories of goods and services: food and water, housing and energy, clothing, health care, transportation, education and child care as well as some money for savings and miscellaneous or discretionary spending.[2]

2 What hours do they work? Can a retailer demonstrate that workers are not subject to excessive overtime or bad terms of employment because of the retailer's supply system?

3 Can workers defend themselves? Are unions and collective bargaining allowed and encouraged in the factories where the clothes are supplied?

Five questions and answers about Fairtrade clothes

The Fairtrade movement began in Europe in the 1960s as a response to growing awareness of worker exploitation around the world. By now you've probably come across Fairtrade bananas, coffee and chocolate in the shops. More recently Fairtrade has moved into the clothing sector and there are now Fairtrade-certified cotton clothes. Fairtrade aims to improve trading relationships with the world's most marginalized farmers and workers. It works with disadvantaged communities to raise incomes, the benefits of which are shared among the community.

What does and doesn't Fairtrade certification mean?

Fairtrade sets a minimum price, based on the actual costs of sustainable production. Buyers also pay a Fairtrade premium – which is set aside for farmers to spend on social and environmental projects or to strengthen their organization. Elected farmer committees decide democratically how these premiums are spent. So for small family farms that rely exclusively on cotton sales for their incomes, in particular, the premium and Fairtrade price can make the difference in covering basic needs such as food, medicine, schoolbooks and tools. Fairtrade-marked items worth almost £300 million are sold annually in the UK, and the Fairtrade Mark is recognized by over 50 per cent of people nationally. By the end of 2006, there were 860 products in the UK using Fairtrade-certified cotton and 27,000 farmers worldwide worked on Fairtrade-certified cotton farms.

So if Fairtrade just guarantees the fair price for the farmers, does that mean a Fairtrade cotton T-shirt could have been made in a sweatshop?

The Fairtrade Mark denotes that the product itself is certified Fairtrade, not the brand name or the retailer. It does not guarantee that the rest of the supply chain has been certified Fairtrade. According to Fairtrade Foundation director Harriet Lamb, over the next three years they will be looking at how to ensure certified standards are applied across the supply chain. However Fairtrade does register all traders along the supply chain to ensure transparency in sourcing. This means that everyone involved – including the spinner, knitter, weaver, dyer, cut/make/trim manufacturer and their sub-contractors – has to respect Fairtrade Trading Standards (for example, through membership of a multi-stakeholder initiative or SA8000 certification), in an auditable supply chain.[3]

What is the difference between Fairtrade, Fair Trade and fair trade?

Only specific products carry the Fairtrade label. Some businesses – including shops and clothing labels – will say they are 'Fair Trade' because they have been certified by IFAT, the global network of Fairtrade organizations, as a Fairtrade business. Using the term 'fair trade' usually means a company wants to assure consumers its products are made by fairly paid workers – although this doesn't mean they are accredited, monitored or verified. They may, however, have set up their own monitoring or auditing system or belong to a multi-stakeholder initiative such as the Ethical Trading Initiative.

Does Fairtrade mean organic as well?

No, although many of the Fairtrade-certified producers groups are also certified organic. Fairtrade producers are expected to implement Integrated Crop Management, which can help farmers gradually convert to organic farming. The most hazardous pesticides cannot be used (see Chapter 3 for information on hazardous pesticides). Fairtrade-certified cotton cannot be derived from GM seeds.

Why don't we have Fairtrade in the West?

This question is asked quite frequently and the Fairtrade Foundation's answer is always the same: Fairtrade was set up to work with developing countries. Having said that, if there were

Fairtrade in the West, the principles would be the same. There is a great deal that could be done to support marginalized societies in Britain. Employment in the clothing and textile sector in the EU fell by 1 million to 2.7 million in 2005 and a further 1 million job losses in the sector are anticipated in the next five years.[4] An alternative would be to search out locally made textiles from producer groups in, say, Cornwall, Wales or the Hebrides.

Can Fairtrade be fashionable?

Six companies are carving a new way of business for fashionable clothing.

Safia Minney, founder of People Tree

Safia Minney has consistently and tirelessly attracted attention to the concept of 'Fairtrade fashion'. People Tree, her clothing company, grew out of Global Village, an organization she started in Japan 16 years ago to work on environmental and social justice issues.

> 'We don't start with the merchandizing board and say this factory will get this series of designs at these prices. We would start with a producer group, see what traditional skills they have, and build it up in terms of these types of fabrics.'

They work with women's groups, indigenous peoples, sometimes even refugee groups. Creating relationships with producers – who receive advice, training and support on developing their skills and their organizations from People Tree – is time-consuming. It can take between three and five years to make it commercially viable.

'It's not a one-shot thing. The typical lifespan of relationship with producers is everything between three and four years, the longest 12–13 years. We can't work with as many people as we'd like because it's incredibly expensive developing the capacity of that group.

'It's difficult – you're competing with fast fashion, you're competing with stuff that costs nothing. The typical garment worker – who will often handspin or handweave our garments – receives about 7 per cent to as much as 9 per cent of the ethically priced value of the garment. This is about 14 times higher, if not more, than a factory-fast produced garment.'

People Tree pay 50 per cent of the cost to producers upfront.

'By our paying 50 per cent advance, nine months before we receive the goods, it enables marginalized people who wouldn't otherwise have access to finance to use that liquidity to pay their people on time at the same time as investing in higher levels of environmental production costs.'

Fairtrade fashion takes a lot of time, effort and investment. Which is why it is all the more surprising that People Tree has a successful collaboration with Topshop, the 'fast fashion' high-street chain known for its low prices and quick turnarounds.

In 2005, they began selling in Topshop's flagship Oxford Street store. The promotion was meant to last one month after being launched during Fairtrade Fortnight; after two years they are still there and twice the size than when they first started. It has helped Topshop answer consumer demand for Fairtrade fashion, but how has it benefited People Tree?

'It's helped to strengthen some of the producers and meet some of the quite strict commercial realities of the British fashion high

*street – in sourcing special types of accessories right down to
the kind of cardboard box for packaging. It's turned up
the pressure.'*

People Tree have a concession in the Whole Foods market in
London's High Street Kensington, their largest to date. Their
newest collections this year include one-off designs by
established fashion designers Thakoon, Richard Nicoll, Bora
Aksu and Foundation Addict. This was their first limited-edition
collection, consisting of 100 pieces per style. It appeared in the
June 2007 issue of Japanese *Vogue*, modelled by supermodels
Helena Christensen, Lily Cole, Shalom Harlow and Anne
Watanabe. They are aiming for similar designer collaborations
in future collections.

'made' jewellery

After many years in mainstream fashion, Cristina Cisilino
founded 'made' jewellery in 2005 – an accessories company
based on traditional African and Middle Eastern designs and
given Western touches from a team of UK-based designers.
Jewellery is handmade by artisan producers using sustainable
local resources such as precious metals, stones and recycled
glass, wood and bone.

Money goes directly to the producers rather than to
middlemen, and a percentage of all profits is invested back into
community projects and further training. 'made' pay all their
craftsmen and women a 'living wage' up to three times higher
than the minimum wage of their home country.

Producers include a team of artisans producing wood, metal
and beadwork in Kibera, the largest inner-city slum in Africa.
George Onyango, a highly skilled Kenyan metalworker,
produces all the logos for the accessories. His work with 'made'

has enabled him to develop his own workshop and double his workforce from four to eight.

UK-based designers include Sam Uhbi, a Kenyan-born designer working predominantly with sterling silver and semi-precious stones, and also horn, bone and shell. She has supplied jewellery to Barneys in New York as well as Harrods and Hennes, and has a 'high profile' client list. Pippa Small – from Wiltshire – has collaborated with Gucci, Nicole Farhi and Chloe. She has also worked on craft initiatives with indigenous communities such as the San Bushman of the Kalahari, the Batwa Pygmies of Rwanda and the Kuna in Panama, helping them to research their traditional designs to generate self-sufficiency and income.

Pachacuti's Panama Hats

Humphrey Bogart, Winston Churchill, Truman Capote … all have fallen for the allure of the Panama hat. Woven by hand from Paja Toquilla straw, a filament split from the leaves of the *Carludovica Palmata* plant, Panama hats are actually indigenous to Ecuador, their association with Panama being a historical misnomer.

Pachacuti, a fair-trade clothing company founded by Carry Somers in 1992, source their hats from Ecuador's women's Panama weavers co-operative. The 400 traditional Panama weavers in the co-operative undertake the entire production process, from weaving to finishing. By cutting out all the middlemen, weavers receive double their previous wages, and profits are used for health care, community development and pensions for elderly weavers.

Fairtrade and organic school uniforms

Somewhat outside the realm of fashion, school uniforms are nonetheless essential pieces of clothing for many, many school-aged children in the UK. A large proportion of school uniforms are made from synthetic materials, and the £1 billion schoolwear market thrives on a workforce that is cheap and expendable. Clean Slate, founded by Mark Rogers and Carry Somers, 'want to do for school uniforms what Jamie Oliver did for school dinners', says Rogers. Their organic and Fairtrade-certified school uniforms range from basic sweatshirts to collared shirts, polo-shirts, girls' blouses, skirts, trousers and pinafores. They also offer a PE kit, which includes shorts, T-shirts and gym bags.

From Kenya with love: Wildlife Works

On holiday in Africa in 1997, Mike Korchinsky saw so much poaching and landscape destruction that he decided to do something about it. He bought a critical area (between Tsavo East and Tsavo West in Kenya) where poaching was rife, and outlined a simple plan: the best way to protect endangered animals is to create a sustainable economic base for wildlife survival. If locals can earn enough to feed their families and send their children to school, and if they understand the importance of the wildlife around them, they won't kill animals – and they'll persuade others to act likewise. In Rukinga, Kenya, Mike created a 32,000-hectare wildlife sanctuary, where elephants, cheetahs and 45 other large mammal species now roam freely.

Next to the sanctuary, an eco-factory was built to produce organic cotton and wool women's wear. Wildlife Works, as Korchinsky's clothing label is called, employs members of the local community, offering them training as seamstresses. In the factory there are four teams of 12–15 people each. At first they were trained to sew T-shirts and vests, then two years ago, with the capsule range, they were trained to sew zips, buttonholes and more intricate techniques. Initially the idea was that the factory would produce 24,000 units a month. The reality is that they now produce 20 per cent of that – but concentrate on improving skills. They pay a 30 per cent premium on the factory's base pay and this amount gets invested back into the wildlife sanctuary. Four new schools have been built, educating 1,200 local children. Local job and community-building is helping to stem the flow of rural unemployed into the slums of Nairobi, and the wildlife sanctuary now extends to over 80,000 hectares – Mike initially bought 32,000 hectares and then the Kenyan government, thanks to its belief in the project, gave them another 50,000 hectares.

Korchinsky is working on rolling out his business model to other countries with critical wildlife areas, using the same principle that wildlife preservation goes hand in hand with creating sustainable livelihoods for local communities. Korchinsky's business partner, Andrew Smith, says:

> 'For every £5 million in Wildlife Work sales, one new eco-factory/wildlife sanctuary, where possible, will be built. One million acres [405,000 hectares] under conservation control represents to us a reasonable achievement and would make a real difference to local communities and to wildlife and their habitats.'

Wildlife Works made their UK launch during London Fashion Week in February 2007. As much as 90–95 per cent of the clothes are made in their own factory, with the remainder being made in Africa. Their wool is from Wales and Vermont, spun from organic yarn. Their next sanctuary will be in Madagascar – to produce outerwear – and the government has already given them a deal to lease land. They also have 16,000 hectares earmarked in Sri Lanka.

MUMO: Making trade fair from the inside-out

MUMO is a new model in 'fashion with responsibility'. It focuses on introducing the best of designer fashion from developing countries to the UK, while ensuring that a proportion of the revenue made in the UK is reinvested down the supply chain to improve the lives of the communities where the clothes are actually made. It focuses on developing already-established labels into being fair-trade products, rather than trying to promote fair-trade clothing as high fashion. And for established designers, becoming eco-friendly is a long-term process.

Launched in November 2006, MUMO is the brainchild of Kirstin Samuel, an ex-banker who, after retraining in International Development, worked voluntarily in Brazil. She noticed the talent of the fashion designers there, and it was then the idea came to her to help their economy by introducing some of the established labels to the UK, but to do so in a socially and environmentally responsible way where possible. Kirstin works out deals with established fashion designers not only to be their exclusive UK agent, but also to agree a contract that sets out a plan and includes milestones to meet on the road to establishing fairly traded supply chains, and to developing and supporting communities.

'The products are "transitional products" which aim to incorporate principles of respecting the environment, and the people who have made the clothes, as normal working practices in the industry. This would ultimately support the certification of the materials themselves together with the factories they are produced in.

'All garments will have a tag saying what we have achieved so far with each designer and this information will also be available on the MUMO website.

'Where we have deliberately used eco fabrics or where we can tell stories about the stage of certification of the factories, we will. The tag will always explain to the end consumer that 5 per cent of revenues goes to supporting this aim. In this way there is a direct link between the end consumer and the development of the entire supply chain, so that together we are building ethical products.'

She has given herself a year until she starts to perform 'audits' on the companies because, although she is liaising with other people in the UK and in Brazil who believe and support the concept, there is a question about how much she can achieve as one person on her own. Ongoing factory visits will take place in Brazil. The process of gaining accreditation wherever possible will also be a continuing one. She has support in Brazil for her endeavours, and has contacts who can help her formalize a process of doing this.

'It is important for us (MUMO) to remember that there are three strands of development going on at the same time: the environment, the people who work to make the clothes, and the supporting communities. To us this is what constitutes an ethical product. The whole supply chain must be considered. This is a long-term commitment and we will need the support of other companies/agencies to ensure transparency and that we are achieving our goals. I believe we have the contacts both in Brazil and the UK to achieve this.'

One of the greatest potential achievements MUMO is setting itself is to work with companies that have scope for changing and improving the way they operate, so as to achieve accreditations for all their factories.

MUMO have plans to open a concept store in London in March 2008.

Currently they represent three labels from Brazil, all of whom show at Sao Paulo Fashion Week:

Zigfreda – is a women's wear line by designer Katia Willie, now in their ninth season. As ex-designer for Maria Bonita she is well respected in the fashion industry in Brazil and consistently creates stunning collections with patterns distinctly recognizable as Zigfreda. Zigfreda care much about the social development of the communities in which they work and have recently bought the factory which produces their collections so that they can have more control over production. Already they pay double the minimum wage (in accordance with the first benchmark set by MUMO) and are working with MUMO on a creche facility project to support the community using MUMO-reinvested revenue.

Huis Clos – one of Brazil's most respected and loved fashion brands. Working with the highest-quality fabrics, often from Europe, they create relaxed pieces with style, and blend neutral shades with fashion-forward colours each season. Huis Clos have a number of programmes working with young people in poor neighbouring areas. Around 30 per cent of the collection is made in-house and MUMO are working with them to gain accreditation for this. There is work to be done with the outsourcing of the rest of the collection, but MUMO see this as a challenge.

Kylza Ribas – touted as the new hot talent emerging from Fashion Rio in recent seasons Kylza has a commercial eye but is able to stay fashion forward while doing this. Again, much of the collection is made in-house with MUMO revenues going towards helping the families of the seamstresses who make the clothes. MUMO are also starting a round of factory visits to begin the accreditation process for the other factories Kylza uses in her production. There is also a plan, as we go to print, to introduce eco fabrics to the next collection.

Chapter 8

Design
pioneers

'This is not about the new colour for spring. It's actually about the new direction of our industry.'
Stella McCartney

Certain designers have been critical in transforming what could have been a trend, into a movement for sustainable style. These designers, some would call them extremists, have been slowly laying the foundations to build this movement – each having carved out their own individual paths for change, from organic to fair trade, to 'reclaimed to wear' and much more.

An eco designer has to contend with a whole host of challenges and difficulties not encountered by other designers: sourcing fabrics, inventing new processes and consciously designing with environmental or social issues in mind. From the consumers' perspective, they add a whole new dimension to appreciating the clothes we buy. Be they campaigners, innovators or thinkers – as a whole, through their work and ideas, they've led to a sea change in the world of clothing and fashion.

Part I: The campaigners

Katharine Hamnett – the queen of eco fashion

Katharine Hamnett's capacity for generating headlines began early in her career. In 1984 she won the British Fashion Council's Designer of the Year award, and she generated controversy by meeting Margaret Thatcher at Downing Street wearing a T-shirt emblazoned with '58% Don't Want Pershing' – referring to the UK public's opposition to the nuclear missiles. Over the last two decades, she has used her slogan T-shirts to raise awareness of issues ranging from HIV/AIDS to the war in Iraq.

But the biggest stir she's caused has been in turning her energies to reforming the same industry that has made her famous. 'You can make millions as a designer, but those millions are being made because you are turning a blind eye to abuse and exploitation of people and the environment,' she says.

In fact, her name is so closely linked to criticisms of the excesses and damage in the fashion world, one wonders whether she is more successful as a campaigner or as a designer. The seeds for her campaigning on environmental issues were sown almost two decades ago when she began research on the impacts of conventional cotton. Shocked to find that the pesticides used in the farming of this 'natural' fibre are responsible for the deaths of tens of thousands of farmers and the poisoning of millions each year, she set about enabling farmers to lead a different life by switching to organic cotton.

'I never thought it was going to be easy. I realized I've got some standing in the industry that I thought I could use to help these people. It was the only thing I could do,' she says. In 1989, she launched a 'Clean Up or Die' collection aimed at raising awareness of the issues.

But in the early 1990s, organic cotton and environmentally friendly dyes and zippers were practically unheard of. Convincing her manufacturers to change their practices to fit her beliefs became one of her biggest struggles. 'Manufacturers think designers are useful idiots,' she says. 'Again and again, with yet another manufacturer, I was told to f*** off with my collection.'

At one point she decided to terminate most of her manufacturing and licensee contracts and start afresh: 'I'll manufacture it myself – I'll put every penny into making this happen to prove it can be done.' Her Katharine E. Hamnett ('e' for environmental) line was hampered, in large part, by the fact that she had to create, from scratch, a new supply chain, and by the surcharges that came with doing this. The sheer cost even of making samples was prohibitive.

> 'It took around £40,000–£45,000 to make trouser samples. I had to purchase 4,000 metres of outer fabric and 4,000 metres of the pocketing as well as 60,000 metres of zip tape for 15 centimetres of a zip. You couldn't get organic fabrics and detailing in small amounts.'

This almost led her to financial ruin, but she decided, 'I'd rather retire to the farm than make my business at the expense of the people who grow and produce your fabrics.'

The result is that she has been an integral part of many developments in eco clothing: from hemp growers in the UK, to organic printers, to NGOs – the list is long and she is always on top of developments.

Katharine now has one of the most eco/ethical collections in existence. Organic cotton, organic zips, water-based PVC-free and phthalate-free printing, vegetable-tanned leather. All the factories she's used have water treatment plants and/or water recycling facilities. The Katharine E. Hamnett line is sold on her website, in Liberty's and on *net-a-porter.com*. It includes T-shirts, sweats, shirts, jerseys, dresses, men's trousers and anoraks.

In February 2006, retail giant Tesco approached her to design a collection for them. Signing a two-year contract, Katharine has designed a line of chinos, sweats, dresses, T-shirts and parkas, called 'Choose Love' for women and 'Saving the Future' for men, which now sells in 40 stores.

Tesco were concerned about the costs of producing such a line, but while the organic cotton farmers benefit from a 20 per cent premium on the price of their cotton, it would reflect only a 1 per cent rise in the cost of the garment.

I asked her whether she thought it was hypocritical to work with one of the companies that had epitomized her grievances against the clothing industry: just-in-time sourcing, bad deals for farmers, cheap, disposable clothing? Katharine's answer is an emphatic no. She wanted to show the industry it's possible, at that price, to have clothes that are stitched to last and beautifully made. For each design she went through three fittings on a model to ensure the cut and drape were correct. It meant prodding Tesco all the while because the cost of this stage was high, but this is where the benefits of good craftsmanship lie.

Packaged in recycled bags, using recycled hangers, the collection was 'virgin territory' for Tesco. A labour rights expert was called in to draft the 'dream contract' for cotton farmers and workers, which includes compliance with fair labour principles.

Through working with Tesco, Katharine has had a greater platform to forward her causes. She is trying to put together a deal involving the UN, the World Trade Organization (WTO), and retailers like Tesco, to create an international certification standard for organic cotton 'in conversion'. For many farmers in Africa organic certification is too expensive, and this prevents them from converting. An intermediate certification that is free to farmers and includes research and support as well as access to a market at the end, would go a long way to swelling the pool of organic cotton on the market.

Her website is as much an online boutique as it is a platform for the campaigns she is involved in, from reforming the cotton market in Uzbekistan to developing concentrated solar power.

Her influence is evidenced in the growing demand, the media exposure and the public awareness of the issues. 'It's just the beginning, it's not time to get self-satisfied or big-headed about anything. I don't see why all cotton can't be organic,' she says.

Rogan Gregory – made in Africa

Bono, the lead singer of U2, has arguably gone a long way to cultivating 'conscious consumerism'. With his RED initiative, which aims to help fight AIDS/HIV in Africa and has rounded up some of the world's biggest retailers – including Gap and American Express in the effort, he has become the rockstar face of activism. Another facet to this is the clothing line Edun (nude spelled backwards) that he set up with his wife, Ali Hewson, and designer Rogan Gregory.

Edun was created in 2005, mainly as a poverty-alleviation project aimed at Africa, giving training and support for the growth of organic cotton and clothing manufacturing. They focus on working with local materials, organic fabrics (as much as possible) and local, fairly paid labour forces.

Edun's ONE T-shirt, is a joint project with the Make Poverty History campaign, and directly benefits HIV-positive apparel workers in Lesotho – providing them with lifesaving drugs.

Edun has helped bring consciousness into clothing consumption. Through their sexy men's wear and women's wear lines, which include tops, bottoms, denims, dresses, jackets and sweaters, they have helped put eco fashion on the pop culture map, while making a difference to communities in Africa.

Stella McCartney – animal-rights activist

Luxury fashion is an industry that relies on leather accessories and fur for a lot of its profit margins. Because of this, it is no easy task to stand up and shout about how they should be made 'ethically' and 'cruelty-free'. But Stella McCartney is the only top-tier designer who has for years consistently refused to use leather or fur. And she hasn't been quiet about it, either.

A prominent animal-rights activist and vegetarian, she reportedly refused to work with leather or fur when offered a job at Gucci by Tom Ford. Instead, Gucci backed her to start her own label, which includes faux-leather totes and shoes and faux-fur jackets. She has said that whenever possible she gets written commitments from her business associates pledging that they will follow her ethical guidelines.[1] She has even challenged British Airways to remove leather seats because of the cruelty to animals.

A long-time supporter of People for the Ethical Treatment of Animals (PETA), she has narrated a video for them which depicts the brutality of animal slaughter, and she is known to lecture friends who wear fur.

Beyond the world of fashion, she has brought luxury to the organic skincare market with her skincare line, Care, developed with YSL Beaute, which uses only organic active ingredients, no GM materials and nothing is tested on animals.

Part II: The innovators

Outdoor enthusiast – Yvon Chouinard of Patagonia

Way before most designers and retailers were even thinking about sustainability issues, Patagonia were producing clothes from organic cotton. And way before others started experimenting with recycled materials, Patagonia were producing fleeces made from recycled polyester.

Yvon Chouinard has been a businessman for 50 years, starting out making iron rock-climbing equipment. His love of the outdoors led his business sense, and his company Patagonia was created to design clothes and gear for campers and climbers like himself. With success and growth coming quickly, the company became 'unsustainable', which led Yvon to rethink their business strategy in the early 1990s.

Using the Iroquois Indians as a model, he decided that business decisions would be made based on seven-generation planning – that is, with a person who represents the future seventh generation in mind. By 1996, all Patagonia cotton clothing was switched over to 100 per cent organic. In 1993, they were the first to start making 'Synchilla jackets' using fibre made from recycled polyester soft-drink bottles.

By 2010, Patagonia aim to make all clothing from materials that have been or can be recycled. Through its recycling programme, it also accepts fleeces made by competitors L.L. Bean and The North Face.

Since 1985, they have given away more than $22 million (£10.8 million) to mainly grass-roots conservational activists, through the Patagonia Foundation. 'We measure our success on the number of threats averted: old-growth forests that were not clear-cut, mines that were never dug in pristine areas, toxic pesticides that were not sprayed,' he wrote in his book *Let My People Go Surfing*.[2]

In 2001, he co-founded 'One Percent for the Planet', an alliance of businesses that contribute at least 1 per cent of their annual revenues to groups on a list of researched and approved environmental organizations.

The shoe man – Galahad Clark of Terra Plana

'To be perfectly honest, I think shoes are bad for you.' Coming from the mouth of a seventh-generation member of the Clark family, the brand which still controls a sizeable share of the UK shoe market and makers of the Wallabee and Desert Boot, this may sound strange. But Galahad Clark's proudest achievement so far is a line of shoes called Vivo Barefoot, designed to feel like you're not wearing shoes at all.

Hand-stitched, using recycled leather, Vivo shoes create a barefoot experience by using an extremely thin, soft, Kevlar sole with finely woven fibres. Normal shoes don't let your feet bend as they were designed to, forcing muscles and ligaments to strain. Vivo Barefoot, on the other hand, 'improves your posture and gives a new natural sensory perception'.

Two of Galahad's ancestors, Cyrus and James Clark, created a small business making sheepskin shoes in Dorset in the 1820s. It grew to become one of the world's largest shoemakers. But by 2006, the last of Clarks 30 factories in England had closed down and moved overseas, though there are still 2,000 Clarks shops in England. Lance Clark, Galahad's father, worked for 45 years in the business. Today, Clarks control 20 per cent of the men's UK footwear market, 31 per cent of the children's and 15 per cent of women's.

Galahad Clark grew up in Clarkstown in Somerset while Lance was at the helm of the company, and he spent summers doing stints in the Clarks factories in England, Italy and Asia. Given this, you might think it impossible to escape working with shoes. But Galahad initially shunned going into the shoe business – instead moving to the US to study Chinese and anthropology at university, then spending a year working in China.

His first experience of designing shoes was a collaboration with the US hip-hop group Wu Tang Clan, who, he discovered, wore Clarks Wallabees. The line was called Wu Shoes.

When a friend of the family approached him with a footwear business, Terra Plana, which was nearing bankruptcy, he jumped at the opportunity. He took over as managing director in 2003. One of his first initiatives was working with Dutch designer Rem

D. Koolhaas (nephew of architect Rem Koolhaas) to launch United Nude, a line of classic shoes, with state-of-the-art wedges produced from fibre-enriched nylon – used in racing cars, never before used in shoes.

After attending an event sponsored by the environmental organization and pressure group Anti-Apathy, he struck up the idea with creator Cyndi Rhodes to make a shoe with recycled materials. Together, in 2005, they launched Worn Again shoes, which are '99 per cent recycled'. Material is sourced, among other things, from recycled firemen's uniforms, hosepipes, Oxfam collection banks, prison blankets and military uniforms. Worn Again give 5 per cent of the value of their sales to Anti-Apathy, and they give another percentage to offset carbon emissions.

The company is run out of the back of one of their two London stores, on Bermondsey Street in east London (they also have two stores in the US and one in Vienna). Every product is graded with their own eco matrix, taking into account materials, efficiency, toxins, packaging, function, emotion-graphic respect and locality. If a product doesn't make the grade then they re-design it or drop it.

For example, a line of ladies' pumps, which used lots of glue was dropped.

Using chrome-free and vegetable-tanned leathers and recycled materials, the shoes also benefit from environmental considerations at the design stage – in that they are constructed in a way that minimizes the amount of glue needed, or they are hand-stitched.

According to Galahad:

'The secret behind selling "ethical" fashion is that 5 per cent of the market will buy it, being eco, regardless of aesthetics, 45 per

cent sit on the fence but could be convinced and the other 50 per cent don't give a f***. We're after that 45 per cent. We like the idea of more than one answer to sustainability. Lots of yeses.'

Clarks sell 60 million pairs of shoes, and Terra Plana a mere 100,000. But Galahad is making a name for himself by carving out his own unique spot in the market. In June 2007, Terra Plana won the *Observer* Ethical Award's very first category for 'Fashion Product of the Year'. An eco Clark on the rise.

The celebrity's designer – Sarah Ratty of CIEL

With her Conscious Earthwear line, Sarah Ratty was one of the original eco design pioneers in the 1990s. She started by cutting up and deconstructing clothes, and radically remaking them into fabulously wild creations. Her first collection was shown in *i-D* magazine and sold in Brown's in South Molton Street, London. Through Conscious Earthwear, she explored working with different types of eco fabrics – from post consumer waste to organic to recycled plastic bottles. The Victoria and Albert Museum acquired some of her outfits for their permanent Dress Collection.

Based in Brighton, Sarah started CIEL in 2003 using eco-friendly fabrics and ethical manufacturing. Sarah's strength is her innovation with the range of eco fabrics and techniques all the while staying 'hip and luxurious'. She has used organic linen, hemp silks, hand-block printing on silk by Indian artisans using indigenous tribal hand-carvings, organic cotton corduroy, organic cotton and bamboo jersey, leather-look quilt using AZO-free dyes and T-shirts with phthalate-free printing.

Previous collections have included cable hand-knit scarves, shrugs, coats and cardigans from traditionally farmed baby Alpaca wool and a range of edgy tailored separates from culottes to skirts and dresses. Constantly mentioned alongside celebrity names, CIEL has done a lot to relieve eco fashion of its sackcloth image, even scooping up the UK fashion export Ethical Fashion Award in 2007.

The incidental environmentalist – Peter Ingwersen of Noir

'It's not more expensive to create beautiful, ethically correct clothing, it's just a lot more of a hassle. If you take an ethical approach you need a different supply chain. But fundamentally you can't persuade people to join in the ethical challenge unless you give them really sexy, stylish clothes. You have to make social and corporate responsibility darn sexy to get people to play the game.'

Peter Ingwersen is an undercover eco designer. He refuses to be defined by a 'green' label and unlike other eco designers, Noir's 'mission statement' isn't as prominent as the clothes themselves. 'I got into designing because I wanted to be a rockstar but couldn't read music. The closest thing was to look like a rockstar,' he says. Peter was a brand manager for Levi's, helping, among other things, to bring to market Levi's twisted jeans.

Peter launched Noir for the Spring/Summer 2006 season. At the same time he created a cotton fabric brand, Illuminati II, the sole purpose of which is to produce the finest sub-Saharan cotton from raw African cotton. Not only can Illuminati II be used in Noir's collections, but it can also be sold onwards to other luxury brands.

Peter has built a long-term relationship with cotton farmers in Uganda, pioneering a supply chain from cotton grown on organic farms in Africa to factories where it is woven in Europe. He has consistently increased the amount of organic cotton used in his own collections, starting out with 30 per cent then rising to 50 per cent and beyond.

Peter also created the Noir Foundation, which allocates the revenue from a percentage of the sales of cotton suits and fabric to support African cotton workers in the supply chain. The Foundation helps to provide essential medicines and micro loans to workers.

From biker jackets, ruffled and fitted shirts, belted trenchcoats, silk and cotton dresses, tailored blazers and long organza evening gowns, season after season his collections have received wide applause from mainstream fashion press. He has put the chic in eco chic.

Ecoture – Deborah Milner

Deborah Milner made her name using unusual fabrics made from unlikely materials. Her creations include sculpted dresses made from plastic-covered wire, strips of film negative and the stainless-steel mesh used in coffee filters. She has now turned her attention to using fabrics 'with a good ethical basis'.

Studying at Central St Martin's and the Royal College of Art, Deborah has a background in couture, and has worked alongside some of the UK's greatest designers, including Alexander McQueen and Philip Treacy. But about seven years ago, she got an itch.

'I became disillusioned with fashion and couldn't find any meaning, yet it is the only thing I know how to do,' she says. She went to Brazil in 2000, and ended up living there for a time. She wanted to get involved in social work and environmental protection, and she finally realized that she could mix these aims with doing what she was best at – clothing design.

She presented the idea of an eco couture line – Ecoture – to ethical skincare giant Aveda, who agreed to finance it in 2005.

'Aveda opened a lot of doors, they paid for the samples and research. Finance stopped at a full-fledged backing of a range,' she says.

In Brazil she had researched and met with an Amazonian tribe, the Yawanawa, with whom Aveda had been working for over a decade. The Yawanawa provide material from the Urukum palm tree, which provides a deep red colour used in their make-up. Through this tribe and the Uruku seed, lots of diverse ideas sprang up for her collection.

Each of the dresses in her Ecoture collection, which was exhibited at London Fashion Week's Estethica exhibition in September 2006, tries to cover the many different facets of 'sustainability'.

For instance, couture often calls for vivid colours, but Deborah found that many of the natural dyes can't provide the same intensity as synthetic colours. The blue of the silk organza 'Small Knot Dress' was created using tree resin extracts and leaf dyes. Working with natural dyeist Penny Walsh, Deborah found that in small amounts there is a wide varieties of colours available. 'When it comes to ready-to-wear then it gets more difficult.'

She received scrap fabric from the leftover stock of Italian silk manufacturer Mantero, maker of luxurious ties (and the exclusive maker of Chanel scarves). The 'Yawanawa Dress' was created using silk duchess satin from these.

Another, the 'Bridal Lace Dress' was made from plastic bags knotted together and then melted on a heat press. This melted the plastic into 'lace', which was then mounted on silk tulle and appliquéd. Though ironing and melting the bags 'started as an experiment, the results were much better than I had expected,' said Deborah.

The 'Sandalwood Dress' was created using silk chiffon

crafted by a women's co-operative in India, and dyed ochre, red and orange using natural dyes made from tree resins such as fustic and madder. The dress's belt, designed by Deborah's colleague Karen Spurgin, is handcrafted from sustainably harvested Australian sandalwood.

What the Ecoture collection gave her was a bank of ideas for a ready-to-wear line. She says that all that is missing is financial backing. Her latest idea is to create a line of eco T-shirts using photos from her trip visiting the Yawanawa tribe, to whom royalties would go. She is also continuing to experiment with environmentally friendly yet unusual fabrics. 'The corset, for example; at the moment there is nothing green about it. Would I be able to find a fabric to make an environmentally friendly corset? Something with a bit of give but really strong.'

The Scavengers – Orsola de Castro and Filippo Ricci of From Somewhere[3]

'We take a tonne of waste and give back a kilo of pride, helping to keep alive Italy's tradition of craftsmanship.'

'Recycling since 1997' reads the motto. In 2006, From Somewhere diverted 2 tonnes of fashion waste from landfill and into the funky, fresh designs of their women's wear collections. It started with Venetian-born designer Orsola de Castro's refusal to throw out a cherished sweater inherited from her grandmother, then evolved into a business customizing second-hand cashmere cardigans retrieved from flea markets and charity shops. Her signature feature was to crochet or sew on buttons or pieces of fabric onto holes or stains.

Her break came when MILES, a famous Italian fabric manufacturer, offered her their damaged goods. Eyeing up their textile waste, she asked for that too. 'I was given anything from production cuts to fabric colour charts. In my mind, they were throwing away gold dust.'

Scouring the rubbish bins of northern Italy undercover wasn't long-lived, as other manufacturers realized that From Somewhere could act as a free waste-disposal service – and give them good PR. 'We started off as a pain in the ass. Now we are providing a service.'

She currently receives rubbish from manufacturers providing for Marc Jacobs, Sonia Rykiel, Valentino and Burberry, to name a few. Sewn together, these offcuts create a wholly unique mix of cashmere, silk, cotton, jersey and tweed, in colourful recurrent themes. 'They are profoundly different but exactly the same,' she says.

Boxes and bits of fabric litter their west London studio. Is there any method to the madness? 'Themed' fabrics are packed up in boxes to send to the seamstresses. One may be filled with different shades of red and brown, or variations of striped blues. The seamstresses are instructed to take certain amounts from specific boxes – so they pick and cut, pick and cut and then assemble, giving them a certain amount of control over the final product.

'We sold 2,000 pieces in 2006. If we ever did 10,000, we might be taking care of all the fabric waste from northern Italy alone. I dread to think about the rest of the world,' Orsola says.

We have Orsola de Castro and Filippo Ricci, From Somewhere's business manager, to thank for 'greening' London Fashion Week. The pair was approached by Hilary Riva and Anna Orsini of London Fashion Week to create an exhibition with the best on offer in eco and ethical design. Estethica (see profile in Chapter 5) is now in its third season and has brought green issues to the attention of the mainstream fashion industry and media.

In 2007, From Somewhere opened up an 'eco boutique' in London's trendy Notting Hill district, designed entirely with 'reclaimed' materials – for example, bike spokes used for clothes racks and 'reclaimed' wood from a local junkyard.

Part III: The thinkers

Slow Clothes – Kate Fletcher

'We need to take a role in transforming the rules and the goals of the bigger industrial system that we are all part of.'

Kate Fletcher's philosophical discourse on the idea of slow clothes paints a picture of what the world of fashion could be, and the many ways it falls short. Kate borrowed the successful Slow Food model, founded by Carlo Petrini in Italy in 1986 – and turned it on the world of fashion. With it, she hopes to help bring about a renaissance in the fashion industry. Slow Clothes, like Slow Food, is about quality of design and production as well as an appreciation of value and quality by consumers.

Fast fashion, Kate believes, is simply about selling more clothes and making more profits.

'Fast isn't free – someone somewhere is paying. Fast Fashion is disconnected from everything from poverty wages to climate change. Slow fashion is not time based, it is about producing, designing and consuming better. It is a new approach in which designers, producers, buyers, retailers and consumers are more aware of the impacts of their products on workers, communities and ecosystems.'

She believes that there can be 'fast fashion' – but with a new agenda. Instead of rampant material consumption, fast could be a creative force. Clothes can be made, for example, using laser technology, or from paper and be put in a compost bin after one or two uses. While she provides ideas on how to make disposable consumption more environmentally friendly, at heart she aims to inspire more emotional attachment to our clothes and to slow down the rate of consumption.

'The challenge of sustainability is bringing about a shift in consciousness. Rather than looking at the symptoms, we need to look at the causes – in part, our addiction to consumption,' she said at a recent conference hosted by the Association of Suppliers to the British Clothing Industry (ASBCI). This comes with replacing quantity with quality in the development and production of garments.

In her view, big change in the world of fashion is possible through design, as design actions are the front end of the lifecycle. 'Design provides vision – it can anticipate and prevent problems and it asks us where we want to be.' Her vision for the future of fashion is inspired by how systems in nature work with efficiency, co-operation and symbiosis. The hope is that society might be sustainable in the same way ecosystems are.

What is at the heart of our consumption culture?

'Most of the world's population actually swims in a sea of clothing, as similarity and lack of diversification leads to boredom and consumption. Just as in food monocultures, we need to use and value diversity and steer away from social monocultures.'

Kate gives lectures and organizes workshops and has carried out consultancy for a wide range of clients – from Marks & Spencer to the Salvation Army.

Rebecca Earley, Chelsea College of Art

'There are no blanket solutions.'

Upcycling; emotional design; long-life – short-life. You or I might not know what these terms mean, but in years to come we probably will, as the design students of today will be the fashion leaders of tomorrow – and they will all be armed with the know-how to put these ideas into practice, thanks to Rebecca Earley.

From 1996 until 2002 she was making handprinted scarves in her east London, Brick Lane studio. After experimenting with heat photograph printing, in 1998 she came up with exhaust printing, a new low-impact print technique which exhausts all the dyes in the process. 'You dye and dye and dye until the water is so clear, it is drinkable.'

At the same time, from 1995 onwards, she was teaching print and design at the Chelsea College of Art. After becoming a research fellow in 2002, she more or less gave up her handprinting, although through research and the exhibitions she organizes at Chelsea she has an outlet for her creative ideas and venues to show her own work.

One of her biggest accomplishments at Chelsea has been opening up the Textile Environment Design (TED) resource centre in 2003. Securing funding to 'buy filing cabinets and hire a research assistant', the TED resource holds the many fabric books Rebecca has collected, with fabric swatches from a wide range of designers – some experimenting with fabrics made from banana leaves, corn and silk hemp. This resource is open both to students and to the general public. With a library, research reports and other information, the TED resource aims to offer assistance, or advice on where to go for assistance, to anyone interested in eco/ethical/sustainable design issues.

Research from the TED resource has been integrated into the curriculum for the BA course in Textile Design, with 60 students entering each year. First-year students work on recycling textiles, putting on an alternative fashion show during the year. Through the 'Short-life long-life' project, second-year students design an outfit illustrating an 'afterlife' for clothes when they are thrown away. Students also consider issues such as natural dyeing or organic clothes.

> *'Instead of radically changing the way you teach, you have to find a way to integrate eco and ethical ideas. It's taken a long time to get the balance right. If you say, "This is a green project", you get appalling work or you don't challenge them in quite the right way. Whereas if you give them the normal brief but integrate the ideas and strategies, you get much better work. In the current "short-life, long-life" show, the work is stunning, and you can't see that that would ever be an eco-thinking brief. You just don't recognize it.'*

She has used research projects to expand on the idea of upcycling, or recycling with an edge. 'The aim is to bring home the idea that we can not only recycle, we can upcycle to make a more stylish product.' Going beyond the conceptual, upcycling could be a new industry in the UK. 'Instead of shipping our recycling overseas, we could have upcycling industries based on the talent we have in the UK. We need to place new designers into these emerging ideas and technologies,' she says.

Another research idea of hers, about creating emotional attachment to clothes, could become a commercial industry. She believes there could be a commercial service whereby people could remake a much-loved but ruined or tattered garment. A website could be created where you could click on various design services, with themes such as leaf prints from the 'Eden project' collection, for example. The individual would be able to keep the garment they love and have a sense of belonging and understanding of the design process of clothes making.

'I know that what we can do here makes a difference when it comes down to designers and their understanding, practice and awareness of these issues and the fact that they are going to be the new crop out into the industry with that knowledge and interest. In 2000, 7 per cent of the student group were interested in writing their dissertations on eco or ethical issues, in this last year it was 67 per cent. I have the biggest pile of marking to do because I have two-thirds of all students' papers.'

David Hieatt of Howies

'There are too many designers and not enough design.'

What may seem like a big sacrifice to other designers, is just plain common sense to David Hieatt, co-founder with his partner, Clare, of Howies. 'Trying to design and make clothes that have the least amount of impact as possible also means doing things better. Striving to continually improve ensures that, even if it comes in inches, today we are better than we were yesterday,' David says.

Making denim, for example, in 'a better way' involved starting from scratch. The normal jeans-making process uses conventional pesticide-ridden cotton, stone washing using lots of pumice stones, which eats away at the natural resource of the planet, then bleaching, over-tinting, adding oil effects, sulphur dyeing and all kinds of nasty chemical treatments.

Howies, on the other hand, use organic cotton; they use natural indigo dyes on a few styles (with the caveat that natural indigo is not a panacea because of the large amount of land needed to grow it); the denim will be eco ball-washed or even unwashed; the jeans will then have only a slight hand brush, if anything at all. One of their styles, the Selvedge denim, is made on a narrow, wooden loom, which means the pairs come out slightly irregular.

'My grandfather was a coalminer, he died prematurely from the job he did. I remember visiting him once and thinking that there was something wrong with the local river because it was clear. It was because the miners were on holiday, so there was no washing of coal in the river.'

This early experience has made David want to 'run a company that we're proud of', which to him has meant becoming aware of the impacts of different manufacturing processes, and then improving on them. 'Manufacturing cotton, an awful lot of stuff is left in the process – where does that go?'

Howies have sweatshirts, zip-up jackets and check shirts all made from recycled cotton. Over 90 per cent of their range is organic and is produced in factories that they've personally checked out or that are used by other reputable companies, such as Patagonia or Marks & Spencer.

'I think designers have never been asked certain kinds of questions before, but we need to think about the end life of clothes when we are designing them. We're probably not going to stop consuming, because we are hardwired that way, so designers need to think about designing for clothes' "afterlife". You never know, it might make for better-looking products in the end.'

With other ideas starting to emerge, such as becoming a carbon neutral company or a clothes renting service, and with all their innovation, David says, 'It's taken us ten years to get to the starting line.'

Chapter 9

Can the high street be green?

S mall-scale, independent designers taking up green causes – producing small collections of clothes for which they can charge a premium – is one thing. But what about the mass market? Can high-street chains, which cater to thousands upon thousands of price-wary customers, with global supply chains and shareholder interests, ever really take up ethical or green issues beyond mere window dressing? The answer is yes, but the degree to which this can be true still remains to be seen.

Three different chains – Marks & Spencer, Monsoon and Topshop – illustrate three different ways that high-street chains can institute change. When senior management takes on the issues, as is the case with Marks & Spencer, it can result in impressive changes. Secondly, Monsoon, a business with very green beginnings, is searching for ways to return to its roots – as commercial success has led them to make many compromises. With the case of Topshop a junior buyer has shown that change can happen from the bottom up, and is an excellent case study in how the retail buyers of tomorrow will help shape clothing retail in the 21st century.

What these three cases share is the fact that they are all keen to be seen as green. With their different core customers and their attempts to keep those customers happy while making their offerings more sustainable, they are proving that sustainability can be mainstream. I had the opportunity to interview Stuart Rose, chief executive of Marks & Spencer, Peter Simon, chairman of Monsoon, and Claire Hamer, buyer at Topshop.

Britain's best-loved 'green' retailer

'If this plan fails, I think it will set the business back and we'll look very stupid. So it won't fail, we'll deliver it.'

Stuart Rose, CEO of Marks & Spencer, referring to Plan A

If you've read a newspaper or magazine, or watched television over the last year, you would have heard of Plan A. If the ad for Marks & Spencer held your attention for more than a nanosecond, you would perhaps be familiar with the slogan that directly follows: 'Because there is no Plan B.'

When talking about 'greening' the high street, it is impossible not to begin with Marks & Spencer. Not because they were the first to take sustainability measures seriously – they weren't. But the sheer scope and reach and ambition of Plan A, launched in February 2007, in one fell swoop eclipsed all other retailers' attempts at grabbing the green spotlight.

And deservedly so. In Stuart Rose, M&S have someone with his finger on the pulse. Britain's favourite high-street retailer had been ailing for years and Plan A is part of a general turnaround – one that can have a massive impact on the rest of the high street.

And speaking of massive, walking into Marks & Spencer's London headquarters, you can't help but notice how Plan A has permeated the whole company. A huge photograph at the entrance shows chief executive Stuart Rose with all of M&S's 500 'eco ambassadors' posing in the shape of the letter A. The eco ambassadors are the green persons in each of their stores whose job it is to be the catalyst to ensure that the store itself is generating ideas to send back to head office. 'Did you see it?' Stuart Rose asks. How could I miss it? 'It took us ages to get them lined up like that.'

The genesis of Plan A

I had heard conflicting reports on the genesis of Plan A so I asked whether it came about after a single eureka moment or was a more calculated decision based on following consumer trends. Stuart Rose explained.

'In truth, it was a bit of everything. In the autumn of 2005, I was increasingly frustrated that a lot of what Marks & Spencer was doing was already quite ethically proper and that we were not getting that message across to our customers. I suppose, to be honest, most of the reason I was concerned about it was there was no point in putting the effort in if you weren't getting the reward for it.

'We had a plan to tell our customers what I call "all the lights hidden under all the bushels" in the business. We came up with this programme called Look Behind the Label, launched in January 2006, which we started plastering around some of our stores. I think there was a lot of resonance from the customers, and certainly people in the business liked it. That was the first bit of it – the business-driven bit.

'The second bit was that I was on holiday reading Al Gore's book and I thought that I ought to let more people have a chance to look at this. We put the film on in November 2006. That accelerated us into "wow, we've really got to do something" stage. We are a business that can do something because we are 99.9 per cent own label, we've had a long history of working with our supply base and with the environment.'

Plan A and beyond

Plan A is a £200 million, 100-point 'eco' plan. The five platforms involve: becoming carbon neutral with minimal offsetting by 2012; reducing the waste going to landfill to nothing on their own operations, and reducing packaging; using even more sustainable raw materials, for example recycled plastic, FSC (Forest Stewardship Council certified) wood, organic wool, cotton and linen; trading more ethically; educating customers on healthy eating.

Q&A with Stuart Rose

Do you plan to trial any eco fabrics such as hemp or Ingeo?

We're looking at them all. I've asked the technical teams to look at any of the natural fibres – it's amazing what's suddenly become fashionable again. But first of all the fibre has got to perform for the right type of garment. Then, because of our supplier network, we can trial it. If it works, it works. If not, then it doesn't.

What about clothing recycling schemes?

We are reusing plastic bottles and turning them into fleeces – the trousers are in stores now, the fleeces will be in store this autumn. We are looking at, ideally, how can you take these goods off people and do something with them. The technology is advanced but it's a sortation thing – you've got to be able to sort the polyester from the natural fibres to do that. But we want to.

What about encouraging people to shop smarter to prevent throwaway consumption?

I think it might be, in the short term, not to encourage people to buy less, but for us to work to find technical solutions to encourage them to buy better. If we tell the next generation, 'You can't buy clothes and have fun with fashion – you're only going to buy one T-shirt a month,' they're going to say, 'Well, hold on, you've had a good time.' We've got to find technical solutions so that you can buy this T-shirt and it's a user-friendly T-shirt. I believe that will happen.

Could the 'Think Climate' clothing re-labelling scheme extend to advising to air dry and only iron if absolutely needed? It could reduce the global environmental impact of cotton garments by 50 per cent.

By the end of the year, we will have 70 per cent of our clothes with a 30 °C wash label in them anyway. Would I go a stage further and say don't tumble dry? Yeah!

What about a carbon report card for clothes? To move on from the air-freighted stickers they put on food. Would you consider that?

In principle, we want to educate the customer. It's no different to us putting GDA [Guideline Daily Amounts] on foods, or indeed to putting traffic lights on foods – red, green and amber. It will happen. But we have to find a way which is universally accepted. There needs to be co-operation across the retail sector and there's certainly got to be co-operation across government. Otherwise we're going to have the same nonsense as we've nearly got now on food labelling, where one manufacturer says do that way, and another does this way – and what do we do? We end up with the consumer just being confused. Government has got a big role to play. The government has been notoriously remiss on coming up with any of the big-picture solutions because they don't want to look as if they're interfering. They are sitting on the sidelines.

From ethical basics to ethical fashion –
an impossible leap?

Marks & Spencer sell 300 million items of core clothing each year. They will be the first to tell you that there are already very high minimum standards on chemical management, labour conditions and animal welfare. Their explicitly eco range of Fairtrade and organic clothes is taking it further. But how far are they willing to go?

Is their aim to take their 'eco and ethical' ranges out of the basics? Stuart Rose's reply is emphatic:

'Yes, to make them more fashionable. You gotta start somewhere. We are one of the biggest cotton users in the UK and T-shirts was the easiest place to start. [M&S have 20 million Fairtrade T-shirts.] But we are looking at introducing organic linen and bringing back wool as a natural fibre. Wool is nature's great wonder fibre and we've let it drift. We are taking eco fashion into the mass market, but we are not forcing it across everything.

'For most women, fashionable will come before the ethical side, especially for younger women. If they have to choose between doing the right thing and looking good, they'll want to look good.

'The most important part of the training that's going on is the technical people and the supplier base. These people must

show us the technology. Unless the fibre performs – whether it's Fairtrade, organic or not – it's going to be no good. The next link in the chain is the designer, who's got to make a garment sexy enough for someone to buy it. The third bit is giving information to our staff to transmit to the consumer to answer questions like, "Why should I pay this?" Or "Tell me the difference between this and this."'

Aiming for more

There is a very commercial purpose to Plan A. In fact, as Mike Barry, M&S environment manager tells me, the results of the Look Behind the Label showed the biggest ever uplift in trust in the M&S brand.

Stuart Rose is unapologetically competitive:

'Our core customer is a little older than other people's, we are bigger in the 35+ than we are in the 25–35 range. Those are the kinds of people who actually now are starting to worry about the world of their own children. The next thing that will happen is that there is peer pressure coming from their children, when they get a bit older and they go to school. The older people have actually got more time on their hands and more money and they are more aware of what's going on so they are pushing downwards, it's the people in the middle we've got to get to.

'The real danger we have now is that we bombard the consumer, confuse them and just turn them off the whole subject – not just of eco fashion but the whole thing, eventually. You know you may lose it for a while.

'All I've done is put some dry tinder together and lit the match. What's happened is the fire is now burning. I hope it's not out of control. People want to do it, what we have to do is stay focused on it. The pressure is on.'

Monsoon: spinning new threads from old yarn

With models Liz Hurley, Lily Cole and Helena Christensen fronting for them, Monsoon have defined the bohemian chic look. With 405 branches in the UK and over 800 branches of Monsoon and their offshoot Accessorize, you'd be hard-pressed not to have one on your nearest major high street. But Monsoon's founder, Peter Simon, got his inspiration not from margins and market share but from small-scale craftsmen working with entirely natural materials. Monsoon is a commercial success now, so the question they need to answer is this: can they be at the same time a successful high- street clothing chain *and* not completely lose sight of their origins as a 'green and ethical' company?

From nudist commune to king of the high street

For Peter Simon it was an unlikely start to a successful career.

> *'I'd had a regular job at a small advertising agency in London and had "dropped out" and went to live on a nudist commune in Ibiza. I was about 21. It was 1969 – a time of "love and peace, man" and "get by on no money". September came and I got cold and really bored doing nothing and I wasn't really a good hippie.*
>
> *'I was selling a type of shaggy woollen coat made in Gozo – an island in the Mediterranean – to Liberty's and on the Portobello Road. Someone introduced me to some clothes that were hand-block printed saris. I've kept that block. [He points to a small segment of a print block on his office windowsill.] I also have one at home. I keep them to remind me of how Monsoon started. I fell in love with the colour, the hand-block printing process. It was the sister of an actor friend of mine who was making these in Rajastan. In all, these types of clothes were being made in villages outside Jaipur and Rajastan.*

'The word "green" didn't exist then, but we were very green. Now that I think of it, we were 100 per cent cotton and silk, using vegetable dyes and using a craft process. It's the only reason I got into the clothing business. I would have never got involved in it, if it involved going to a factory; but I was out in the village in India or travelling overland.

'I took on the selling of these clothes in England. I said to the people I was working with at the time, "We've got to have a shop." We were being messed around by department stores, we were never gonna go anywhere unless we had our own place. We were vertically integrated – virtually unheard of at the time. I said, "We're going to go from Jaipur to Knightsbridge and no in-between."

'They didn't want to come along with that vision but that was my vision. That's when Monsoon was started, as a shop in Beauchamp Place in Knightsbridge. It was an accident. Somebody who was helping me at the time was on their way to an appointment and she broke down in a car in Beauchamp Place. She phoned me to say the car had broken down on Beauchamp Place, "And by the way I'm phoning from a shop and it's for sale." It wasn't chosen consciously.

'The shop traded for a few months without any name. I wanted a name that was not English. In the end I chose a name that I was associated with, because I was actually born in a monsoon in Sri Lanka.'

Thirty-five years later

So 35 years ago, did Peter Simon ever imagine he would be the chairman of a successful high-street brand with 800 shops?

'At the time all I was worried about was "Am I going to go bust next week?"

191

'For a long time all the clothes were from India. Originally the clothes were Raj-type designs, traditional designs from Rajastan in hand-block printed fabric which was from saris. They were quite ethnic designs. It was aimed at a very small group of people who could carry it off and had the confidence to wear it. There was a lot of quilting involved because it was all cotton voile. So you had strange Lady So-and-so with a castle in Scotland wearing it because the quilting was "wonderful in this draughty castle". But the main thing was it was all very natural.

'We couldn't really stay like that for long. We started opening up a lot of shops, and it was too tight a band. And we had nothing for winter – there was no wool, we had only cotton. We were driven to find fabrics. By this time we had a designer. We had to have something other than our quilting cotton in winter. We then went on and got wool out of China.

'We have never had a factory, I've never wanted a factory. I've always felt you should specialize in what you are good at. We have stayed loyal to our core customer, continuing with block printing or batik, hand embroidery and beading and a lot of craft-orientated product. But we have had to make changes. For a start, some of the vegetable dyes you can't use any more – because of the scale of our operations, and because they ran, and they faded. I remember us doing a bikini which was hand-block printed, and putting a Dry Clean label on it – it was crazy. There were practical issues.

'As we got bigger we had to compromise. Our designers needed different fabrics and we went into evening wear and the range got wider. We were also taking on bigger and bigger leases on the high street. The range evolved, and as it evolved it could no longer stick to 100 per cent silk or cotton and handcrafted.

'I think the mistake we've made is where designers have tried *to chase fashion trends. I think they should reflect their version of them, but their core should be directed at their customer and what they are about. When designers go off on a tangent, that's where it goes wrong.'*

Reckoning with their roots

Monsoon's core customer is between 25 and 35, intelligent, a working woman or mother. She is somebody who wants something different, and who may only occasionally shop in high-street chains. She appreciates fringe, colour or texture. Somebody who travels and is quite open.

Many of the biggest names on the high street have taken on the green image but Peter Simon says, 'In a way, we were there even before Body Shop. I don't think we've communicated very well where we've come from. But we've always been there. All the chains have gone to India because it is a cheaper source for clothes. But we were there from day one.'

While Monsoon were 100 per cent in India in the early days, now they are about 30–40 per cent in India. They have an office in Delhi, with about 40 staff who are there to monitor the people Monsoon work with. They check that everything adheres to their Code of Conduct, and they carry out audits. Monsoon use independent auditors as well.

Monsoon's green initiatives

At Monsoon there are three main 'ethical/eco' aspects: their involvement with the Ethical Trading Initiative, of which they are a founding member; the Monsoon Accessorize Trust, launched in 1995, which aims to help improve the lives of disadvantaged women and children in Asia and which will distribute around £150,000 in donations in 2007; and their support for London Fashion Week's ethical fashion exhibition Estethica, they are the sponsors of the September 2007 London Fashion Week and February 2008 seasons.

Q&A with Peter Simon

How can you ensure labour, health and safety standards are adhered to with your overseas supply chains?

We do our best, nothing is perfect. We hear of things every now and again but we have a very straightforward system where, as soon as we hear of it, we do something. We find out what's wrong, we give assistance where we can, we don't just strike the supplier off, because they are employing a lot of people. We try to tackle things as they come and we try to improve every year.

I definitely think our suppliers have improved. We don't go for the cheapest – we are still working with our very oldest suppliers. I can name you six that we've been working with for over 20 years and one or two we've been working with for 35 years. We don't just say, 'Hey, it's cheaper in Bangladesh, goodbye.'

What about reducing your carbon footprint?

In May 2008, we're moving into our new headquarters, which is an 'eco office'. It includes rainwater harvesting and was designed to minimize the energy use; it's as green a building as you're going to get. We have plans throughout the company to reduce our emissions – with a goal of reducing our air miles by 30 per cent over two years by shipping by sea; and we've cut out plastic bags at Accessorize. [Monsoon have always used paper bags.]

What are you offering in terms of Fairtrade and organic clothes?

We have a small Fairtrade cotton range, and are trying very hard to source Fairtrade silk but the standard doesn't yet exist. The process by which silk is woven, in Bangalore in particular, you can see the conditions in which it happens: they are using children to do it, they want to keep the heat out so there is no light, so the children's eyesight goes very quickly. I wanted to do it right away, because we've used silk from the beginning – but there is no certification. We hope to pioneer it.

We started off with a small range of Fairtrade cotton. Rather than have some token range in the corner of the shop, I'd prefer it to grow naturally and come into our main range and have the designers be turned on by it and want to work with those fabrics. There is also the idea of sponsoring new designers at London Fashion Week's Estethica, to help support budding eco designers perhaps use these fabrics. This is something which we identify with immediately. In the past we've supported designers that are now very well known. Matthew Williamson had his first job at Monsoon, Rufat Ozbek also had his first job here, and Betty Jackson.

Green roots vs. greenwash

How far are Monsoon willing to take their ethical initiatives?

'I think what's happening at the moment is that the consumer – for the same reasons that were there in the early 1970s when Monsoon started – is pushing it forward. The consumer has a guilt thing: there is a huge divide between the rich and the poor, a lot of people are travelling now and see a lot of poverty, there is the climate issue. There are a lot of things going on. In a way the consumer, I think, wants a value-added comfort factor when they make a purchase, and now that extends to clothes. This time it is definitely a consumer pull instead of a supplier push.

'We have big challenges now. One is that our cost base is much higher than others'. There is a group of very low-priced competitors, Primark, Asda, Tesco, and they are selling things dead cheap. How are they getting it so cheap I am not going to say. It is very difficult to compete with them on that. But I'd like to think we are offering a different-value product and that the people working directly or indirectly for us are in better living conditions. But it is very difficult to keep our prices from not going up.

'To have ethically produced clothes, organic cotton, Fairtrade cotton to Fairtrade silk is really very much part of our heritage anyway. As is colour, texture, embroidery. I think we should be different – some people do tailored looks, or without colour – but I want to have that edge. It distinguishes us commercially.

'I don't want in any way to preach a green cause. Monsoon is a commercial organization, we are out there to be as competitive as possible. I'd like to think we are doing good things – but that is something separate. But I would like our customers to feel that they can trust us, they can trust what they are buying – the quality, the fabric and they've got something different.

We'd like to assure them we are doing more than just the minimum when it comes to ethical trading.'

Junior buyers: Topshop's ethical initiatives – from the bottom up

Arguably, retail buyers are one of the most influential groups of people involved in the growth of the ethical fashion market. They are the direct link between designers and consumers. Claire Hamer, a junior buyer at Topshop, was instrumental in getting Topshop to stock their very first Fairtrade clothing line, People Tree, and to create their own line of Fairtrade clothes.

'I've worked for Topshop for three and a half years. At Topshop buyers are quite key. It's our decision as to what gets puts in stores. In a lot of stores it's designer-led. At the end of the day, who's going to make the product and where it's going to be made, is down to the buyer.

'My proper job is buying leather handbags and belts. I'm not an "ethical buyer", the term doesn't exist. I started the whole Fairtrade thing when I was in the jersey department on cotton a year ago. I was looking into how harmful the cotton industry is. It's not the natural product we think it is. A lot of customers have no idea at all. I first wanted to do a yoga range that was organic, but my belief is in poverty reduction, to ensure people have their basic needs taken care of and have access to an education.

'When we first spoke to the Fairtrade Foundation, they were beginning to launch the cotton mark in 2005 in stores. We were working with them on getting Fairtrade accreditation for our own brand of Fairtrade wear. As a member of Arcadia, they wanted to make sure we were committed and so it took a year and

a half to get accreditation. I didn't want to sit around, so we decided on putting People Tree in our flagship Oxford Circus store.'

People Tree's concession at Topshop was launched during Fairtrade Fortnight in 2006 and was meant to last for just a month. After a year and half they are still there and are twice the size they were when it first started. Topshop have also collaborated with them to produce a 'People Tree for Topshop' line. Clare explains:

'The idea was to move this whole Fairtrade thing forward. They've got the supply chain know-how and we've got the design skills – let's think of something together that's simple but young. Once we realized it was going to work, we didn't want to wait another six months or a year for another collection. We decided we'll have it coming in every three months, which is what we do now. It gives them a new customer base.'

Fairtrade fashion – breaking the Topshop mould

Fairtrade is predicated on taking time and effort to support and develop community groups in developing countries. As such, can it ever play a role in the world of fast fashion?

'Fairtrade fashion works differently than normal. As a buyer you'd see a jersey T-shirt and say, "Right, beautiful, I'm going to buy anything between 500 or a million pieces." Depending on where you get the cotton from, it could take anywhere from three to four weeks to three months.

'With Fairtrade cotton, it's like having to put your money where your mouth is months prior. It's a completely different mindset. In reality, you need to plan a year and a half in

advance. How the hell in a fashionable company are you supposed to know a year and a half in advance what type of garments people are going to want to be wearing?

'People say, "Oh well, why isn't the rest of the store Fairtrade?" These are small cottage industries, they are not factories. You couldn't turn around and say, "Right, I want 10,000 knitted scarves." You'd have to give them two years' notice.

'We don't do any promotions for the Fairtrade stuff. As soon as you start shouting about something, you just attract people who slag you off. I'd love to shout about it, but you've got to be careful, and take it slowly. We need to use our own supply chain and try and change that at the same time. Fairtrade is about giving the customer a choice.'

Topshop's ethical initiatives

Aside from stocking Fairtrade fashion brand People Tree, and their own expanding line of Fairtrade clothing, Topshop stock a Fairtrade baby-wear range including brands Gossypium, Hug and People Tree.

Topshop have also recently launched a Corporate Social Reponsiblity programme. This is a three-year programme and each year Topshop will publish a report telling people how they're doing. They will welcome feedback. However, the details of the goals they set themselves are not on the website.

Young, hip and ... ethical

Clare says the rest of the team at Topshop were very supportive of the idea of a Fairtrade range and she personally didn't encounter any resistance.

'As a buyer, you're free to be creative and everyone's opinion is valued. We are such a big company we are able to trial things. But I've been very lucky because everything we've done that's Fairtrade has done really well.

'M&S are buying millions of basic Fairtrade T-shirts, but I don't want to do basic T-shirts. We now have something that is in all our stores around the world, which is a boyfriend turnback cap-sleeved T-shirt across five colours, two with motifs. I'm really proud of that, I think it's fantastic. It works for us and the supplier. To really open it to the masses and change mindsets we need to get fashionable products that are exciting.

'We get inspiration not only from catwalk shows. We get inspiration from around the world. We shop a lot. By the time the catwalk shows come out, we've already done quite a lot of the season, because we bring out all their clothes before their actual real things come out. What they show on the catwalk won't come out for another six months, whereas we get ours out pretty much straight away.

'Topshop is a platform for newcomers and everything that is at the forefront of what is happening. Our generation is in a position where we love spending, we can still do what we love, but we can think about it in a different way. We can't just change overnight. The customer is savvy, they know what they want, but they're dictated to by the media. Magazines like Grazia *coming out every week saying things like 'must buy of the week'. I think the whole thing needs to slow down. But if Topshop said we're going to change, then someone else will take our place, unless there is a pact between us all.'*

Timeline of UK high street organic and Fairtrade lines

- Asda/Wal-Mart introduced a line of organic cotton men's and ladies' T-shirts in April 2007. Their organic cotton George baby-wear line is about to launch.

- H&M introduced organic cotton during March 2007 in all 60 UK stores as well as their stores in 26 other countries. This collection includes women's dresses, tunics, blouses and jersey tops teamed with leggings, sweatshirt couture pieces, a bra and hot pants. The Swedish retailer dabbled with organic in the 1990s, but the lack of consumer awareness and high costs of organic cotton derailed that effort. Their children's wear collection three years ago included plain organic cotton babygrows and T-shirts, but the collection was small and, according to spokesperson Chloe Bowers, 'unfortunately there was not a press release'. The 2005 Stella McCartney for H&M collection carried one organic T-shirt. Their goal is to use 600 tonnes of organic cotton in 2007 compared with nearly 30 tonnes in 2006. For the past five years, they have worked with the World Wildlife Fund and Organic Exchange to promote organic cotton.

- Nike has set a goal of using at least 5 per cent organic cotton in all of its cotton products by 2010. In 2006, 52 per cent of its cotton products reached the 5 per cent threshold.

- Next launched their first organic cotton range during 2006 and increased the collection for Spring/Summer 2007. They are continuing to develop the range for Autumn/Winter

2007 across four product areas. In 2007 they also developed their first range of Fairtrade Mark cotton children's T-shirts, men's and women's socks, and children's bags. Both the organic cotton and Fairtrade cotton products are available from the Next Directory, online and through their approximately 230 stores nationwide.

- The Gap launched an organic cotton men's T-shirt in March 2007 in their US stores. In the UK, they launched a babyGap range of organic cotton bodysuits and hooded jackets. According to spokesperson Fiona Robson, 'Gap continues to explore the use of Fairtrade cotton and hopes to introduce additional items made with organic cotton in coming seasons, but we have nothing further to announce right now.'

- Primark launched a range of organic cotton T-shirts in early 2007. According to spokesperson Helen Penney, 'There are four styles in various different colours plus a boob tube. The T-shirts are either plain or printed and prices start at £4 for them to £5 for the boob tube.'

- Tesco launched a range of organic cotton clothes designed by Katharine Hamnett in early 2007, and this is detailed in Chapter 8.

Chapter 10

DIY fashion

A Saturday afternoon patching up a hole in a beloved sweater or taking up a skirt's hem may not seem like a Saturday well spent. For a variety of reasons, the self-sufficiency once so valued in generations past now seems outdated and unnecessary. This is a shame, because mending, sewing, refashioning and the like are weapons in an arsenal of skills on how to revitalize and individualize a dulling wardrobe. Even those among us with the most bulging clothes racks at some point wake up and find that they have 'nothing to wear'. Instead of rushing out to buy something new, giving old clothes – whether your own or someone else's – a second lease of life can be more satisfying and add to a more distinct wardrobe.

Seven tips to relieve closet boredom

1. Refashion

'. . . fashion is about today. You can take an idea from the past, but, if you do it the way it was, no one wants it.'

Karl Lagerfeld

Designer Karl Lagerfeld used to haunt flea markets and thrift shops for vintage dresses, taking them apart to learn the secrets of their construction and design. A lot of designers look to historical references and pair them with contemporary trends to make a distinct look. As much as the industry is focused on the future, there is always a nod to the past.

The same idea can be applied to our own wardrobes – and you don't need to match Karl Lagerfeld's skills to transform an out-of-date, outsized or tattered garment that you once loved into a brilliant new item in your wardrobe.

Eithne Farry, author of *Yeah, I Made it Myself* is an expert in no-sew sewing techniques and has been refashioning her own clothes for many, many years.[1] I went to meet her and took a bag of my own worn-out clothes that, for one reason or another, I refused to give away, to ask for ideas on how I could bring them back to life – and the results were very impressive.

- A sari I bought years ago for an Indian wedding – turned into a stylish beach kaftan with a snip of the scissors
- The Paul & Joe silk chiffon shirt that was way too big – reborn using a pretty green ribbon to pull it in
- The wool sweater I could no longer wear but would not throw out – felted to become a winter handbag
- The denim pregnancy skirt with a huge elastic waistband that didn't even fit well when I was pregnant – 'No problems. It'd be a cinch to replace the waistband and hem it in. You could even add some embroidery.' I did as she said and have been wearing it ever since.

For many people, time and money are the two things that prevent them from embarking on adventures like this. Eithne has proved that it need not involve much of either, and her book gives simple instructions on everything from making felt handbags and other accessories from our 'unwanteds' to customizing or updating skirts, dresses and jumpers.

The next time you feel your wardrobe simply doesn't offer anything worthwhile you can use it as an opportunity to sort out the clothes that you haven't worn in, say, a year, and put them aside. Consider how these clothes can be refashioned – either into something entirely different, or something fresh just with a new hemline or a change of buttons. This pile of clothes may not disappear overnight, but will provide a worthwhile project for rainy Saturday afternoons.

Clothes surgeries

Kerry Seager and Annika Sanders started Junky Styling in 1997 after witnessing the booming textile recycling markets in cities such as San Francisco and Tokyo. Junky Styling have made a business of deconstructing second-hand clothing and reworking it into new, unique garments. Their signature men's and women's line is produced from recycled suits, coats and wools.

Aside from their off-the-peg collection, Junky Styling have evolved to offer a Wardrobe Surgery service, giving customers an opportunity to bring in favourite garments that are out-of-date or damaged, to be reworked into new, made-to-measure designer creations. Their aim in this is clear. Kerry says, 'I'd like to see less waste in general, and a movement away from such seasonal designs.' Junky don't conform to fashion trends, instead they promote original designs that have longevity.

Recycle Your Jeans is another clothing surgery – this time taking in old blue jeans and transforming them into Denim Kalahari sandals. The parent company of Recycle Your Jeans is Softwalker Ltd, one of a very small handful of shoemaking companies still manufacturing in the UK. Their factory in Cumbria was originally one of many around the country owned by K-Shoes, which was later taken over by Clarks Shoes. After shoe production was shifted overseas the factory was bought by the current owners, Mike and Lynne Stables, who rehired many of the K-Shoes staff.

A stitch in time saves nine

'We need to reinvent the desire for repairing and remaking.'

Rebecca Earley, Chelsea College of Art

Ultimately, whether or not we bother to have the clothes in our wardrobe mended or repaired is a mark of how much we value them – but in the long term, cost savings will definitely be made by spending on the upkeep of more expensive but better-quality classic clothes that last year after year, rather than buying cheap disposables that are constantly having to be replaced.

Each of us in the UK spends, on average, about £625 a year on clothes. But how much do we spend when these clothes need repair? Only 2 per cent of our clothing budget goes to cleaning, repair and 'hired' clothes. There is more than one reason for this. For one thing, if a pair of trousers cost £15, what's the point of spending money on repairing or cleaning them when you can practically get a new pair instead?

This economic argument is coupled with the fact that there's been a marked decline in the number of tailors, cobblers and dressmakers to fall back on when clothes do need expert repair. Thirdly, it's no longer the case that every household has a sewing kit or just a simple needle and thread to quickly replace buttons or patch a sweater. While there's been a resurgence in knitting and sewing (see below), what used to be considered a useful skill, and even taught in schools, still conjures up, especially for women, images of mid-20th century, pre-women's liberation drudgery.

Lastly, given a choice between 'mended' (but 'as good as new') or 'new!', many people are drawn towards the new. This perhaps touches on wider issues in our culture, in which having the most up-to-date and new is a way of keeping up with the times.

2. Accessorize

Waking up any wardrobe can be as simple as pairing together a funky belt with a classic little black dress. Mary Fellowes, contributing fashion editor at *Vogue*, gives her top tips.

(i) Make sure you have some timeless basic staples in your wardrobe that don't date and work well with accessories. These could include:
• black drainpipe trousers
• loose V-neck T-shirts in black, white, cream, nude pink and grey
• simple A-line dress and/or shirt dress with no print, either shift or T-shirt sleeves or long sleeves, in the same colours as above or any colours that suit your skin tone
• plain cashmere V-necks and grandfather-style cardigans in both hip length and extra long (oversized)
• classic black gym plimsoles
• pair of classic round-toed, knee-length boots, either high-heeled or flat, in leather or suede

(ii) Accessorize with these to keep your look up to date:
• big chunky necklaces, big chunky bangles – the quirkier the better
• long skinny silk scarves, plain colours
• quirky/kitsch ankle socks
• colourful and quirky belts – not worn on hipster jeans

(unflattering because they break up the body unless you're a size 8); best worn over long knits/A-line; vintage is fine – 1960s or earlier; otherwise modern
- shoes – make sure you can walk in them
- hats – vintage hats are good but avoid clichéd, mainstream, high-street hats like the classic sunhat and the beret (they look so unoriginal)

Don't bin it, bag it

Plastic bag factfile:

- On average, we use each plastic bag for 12 minutes before discarding it.

- Up to 47 per cent of windborne litter escaping from landfills is plastic – much of it plastic bags.

- Plastic bags do not biodegrade, they photodegrade – break down into smaller and smaller bits, contaminating soil, waterways and oceans, and entering the food chain when ingested by animals.

- Plastic bag litter is lethal in the marine environment, killing at least 100,000 birds, whales, seals and turtles every year.[2]

- Most of the carrier bags used in Britain are made in factories in China and travel halfway around the world to be dished out on our high streets; many are then shipped back to be recycled.[3]

Fed up with plastic shopping bags?

Using plastic shopping bags seems so silly when the easiest thing is to invest in a stylish reusable shopper bag. Aside from Anya Hindmarch's 'I'm not a plastic bag', which sold out within hours of going on sale in April 2007 and is worn by various celebrities, there is a wide range of alternatives to plastic bags.

Onya Bags, made of parachute material, are light and yet strong and highly durable; and they are packed in a little pouch, so can fit into a handbag. They come in a huge range of colours and retail for about £6.50.

Hemp and jute carrier bags – made by a variety of companies – are beginning to be offered for sale by more and more shops as retailers have agreed to reduce the environmental impact of their carrier bags by 25 per cent by the end of 2008.

3. Charity shop chic

Dark, dusty and full of undesirables they are not! Charity and second-hand shops have been dusting off their unfashionable images following the growing trend for alternatives to high-street shopping. While in the past you may have had to be brave to trawl through racks and piles of not-so-carefully arranged goods, today's shops try to rival the 'normal' shopping experience by offering pre-selected racks of clothes of only the best-quality goods – by either style, quality or label. Most neighbourhoods will have more than one second-hand shop, and an attractive window display of goods is usually a good indicator of the quality of the shop's stock and the 'fashion sense' of the staff. Many second-hand shops have goods that are brand new, and garments with stains, rips or any damage aren't allowed on the shop floor. Two chains are particularly notable: TRAID and Oxfam.

Textile Recycling for Aid and International Development (TRAID) is a charity committed to protecting the environment and reducing world poverty by recycling and campaigning. TRAID operate over 900 textile recycling banks across the UK. They divide the funds received through the collection and sale of reclaimed clothing and shoes between providing emergency aid and supporting sustainable projects overseas. In 2006, TRAID donated £58,716 to five overseas development projects focused on health, livelihoods and youth.

Through their eight shops around the UK, TRAID are known for their designer bargains, exclusive one-off pieces, vintage and high-quality brand names. What's more, through their own recycled fashion label, TRAIDremade, clothing that is torn or stained is reconstructed and redesigned by a group of designers who work exclusively with donated materials to produce completely one-off and original pieces available for purchase in TRAID's Brighton shop and in four of its London shops.

Oxfam has around 750 shops in the UK. The fact that Jane Shepherdson, former head of Topshop, recently became Oxfam's new retail advisor, can only bring a much welcome boost to the chain. Aside from their various collaborations with designers such as Stella McCartney (who designed a vest top for sale at the Glastonbury Festival) to make high-end clothes accessible to more people, their 'Oxfam Originals' shops specialize in vintage and retro clothing and cater to more fashion-conscious shoppers. All the clothing, shoes and accessories donated are carefully sorted to ensure you get good quality at a fair price. All of the profit made from Oxfam shops helps to fund their work in more than 70 countries.

As of September 2007 you can buy from Oxfam's online shop. It includes donated items – clothes, music, books and collectables – as well as Oxfam Unwrapped Gifts and Fairtrade products.

4. Shop vintage

Anita Bott has always loved clothes. She was often found
rummaging through her mother's collection of second-hand
'one-offs'. This led later in life to a habit of scouring charity
shops for distinctive clothes, which she would mix with high-
street items to create her own individual look. 'I love the fact
that you can have a piece that is so unique, and the quality of
clothes made 30 or more years ago is so much better than today,'
she says.

Anita is talking about vintage clothes – strictly speaking,
vintage fashion is clothing that dates from the 1970s and before
(non-purists consider 1980s to be vintage). Items newer than
that are simply considered second-hand, and clothes that
pre-date the 1920s are known as antiques.

As Anita realized the extent to which vintage had an appeal –
not only to 'fashionistas looking for originality but also to our
increasingly eco-friendly society', she started to organize a sale of
her own, and the Battersea Vintage Fashion Fair was born.

In a 1970s town hall in Battersea, her Vintage Fair started off
with 35 stands and now has 62, with vintage dealers coming from
all over Europe. Her Vintage Fair is like having over 60 vintage
shops in one place, and can offer a multitude of bargain buys.
Other places to buy vintage include auction houses (Christie's
and Sotheby's both have vintage auctions), car-boot and garage
sales, flea markets and the internet.

Anita says that the average spend at her fair is £75–£100 for a
high-quality vintage dress. She says that when shopping for
vintage there are a number of things to bear in mind:

*'You must try things on. Back then people were smaller, so the
sizes on the tag don't reflect today's sizes. Also be on the lookout
for stains, rips or other damage – you need to look at the piece in*

good light. One of the best ways to wear vintage is to mix and match old with new – there is no point looking like you stepped out of a period drama – you can mix a 60s smock dress with contemporary heels and accessories.'

She says that it does take a bit of confidence to wear vintage, but that people who buy vintage tend to be trendsetters.

Key finds of her own include a 1960s white tasselled minidress for £60 and a 1950s pink satin and lace ballgown for £75, which she said would be worth £1,000 if bought new. 'The great thing is, I can see my daughters wearing it. The dresses will go round and round.'

Reference books on vintage are Funmi Odulate's *Shopping for Vintage*, and Christa Weil's *It's Vintage, Darling!*[4] eBay has an impressive vintage collection; sellers can give the proceeds of auctions straight to charity.

5. Clothes swapping

Swapping is a means to offload all the clothes in your wardrobe you don't want while at the same time being able to pick up high-quality fashion pieces for bargain prices, all in a social atmosphere.

With parties such as Swap-a-Rama Razzmatazz, founded by Eloise Markwell-Butler and now a regular event at east London restaurant Favela Chic, or online portals such as *www.whatsmineisyours.com*, set up by stylist Judy Berger, which allows its thousands of members to swap clothes and furniture, swapping hasn't brought about an end to shopping, it has simply made it more fun and personal.

'Swishing' is another concept making headway, originated by the sustainable PR agency Futerra. Their own swishing events have introduced the idea of 'ecofabulousness', which combines fashion with green ideals. Futerra's Lucy Shea says that swishing was born in a moment of collective inspiration on one of Futerra's away weekends. With swishing, they are trying to make sustainable development 'so desirable it becomes normal. It's about being beautiful on the outside, green on the inside.' Their parties preach light-hearted sermons on the benefits – environmental, social and ethical – of clothes swapping while creating a lively, fun and alternative shopping experience. 'It can get quite elbows out, so we jokingly advise "no scratching or biting",' Lucy says. As well as in London, swishing events have now been organized in Cardiff, Gloucestershire and Wiltshire, and their website, *www.swishing.org*, allows you to download swishing party invitations and instructions.

6. Dresses for hire

At the moment, leasing is not common for personal clothes, but is well known for uniforms, working clothes, costumes, wedding outfits and maternity wear. But this may all change as the benefits of leasing clothes are made more apparent. According to a study by the Institute for Manufacturing (IFM) at the University of Cambridge, leased clothes offer a wide range of styles and sizes, while relieving the burden of storing clothes at home. Environmentally speaking, leasing leads to clothes being used more intensively, thus reducing our total demand for virgin materials for new clothes.[5]

As attitudes to clothing have changed with the rise of disposable clothes, leasing allows fast change-over of garments, worn only a few times by each person, without the need for fast disposal. The market for leasing is underdeveloped, but IFM's eight-week study found that retailers could make a profit from the leasing of certain kinds of garments.

7. Make your own clothes

'When a woman learns to sew, she becomes more fashion-conscious than if she just goes out and buys what she wants.'

Mrs Hubert Humphrey, wife of former US Vice President

'I love the patterns and the colours and the drape of different fabrics and that's just the cloth. That's before you get to the top stitching on a set of bed linen, the buttons, the bows, and of course the cut of a garment silhouette and its corresponding pattern piece.'

Abigail Petit, Gossypium

'My mother and sisters were always knitting. I grew up with it. The first thing I knitted was a Doctor Who scarf when I was about 12. I started off as a knitwear designer. American Vogue *called me "the king of the cobweb".'*

Designer Julien MacDonald[6]

Kate Buchanan got into knitting in her teens, during the last big knitting revival in the early 1990s. She learnt to knit using patterns in a knitting magazine, and throughout university and upon entering the workforce she was always 'messing about with bits and pieces'. Stumbling across a knitting circle website, she was struck by photos of women knitting in a public café. 'At the time meeting in public was quite new. It was a bit funkier than the traditional image of knitting circles where you sit around drinking tea at people's houses.'

She liked the idea so much she started her own knitting group in west London almost four years ago. The group meet once or twice a month in Ealing and there is no entry fee. 'All I ask is that, because it is a public place, people at least buy a drink,' she says. With varying degrees of knitting skill, the more skilled in the group lend a hand to those with less experience.

'I like the atmosphere, it's very fun and friendly. It's also addictive – the gentle, repetitive movement of knitting puts your brain in relaxed state. I think it's in our nature to be creative, and it's great to see the look of joy on someone's face once they've made something.'

Kate says one of the best things about knitting is making something that you couldn't have bought in a shop. 'At the moment I am making a jumper with a kind of leaves texture running across the sleeve, it's totally unique.' While Kate has taken knitting to an extreme – teaching classes and designing her own patterns, even knitting 'on trains and in front of the telly' – she says anyone can learn how to knit after one lesson as there are only four stitches: cast on, knit, purl and cast off. There is an unbelievable range of textures and materials on offer and a full-sized adult garment can be completed in from 20 to 50 hours, depending on your level of skill.

Postscript

S hopping may be satisfying, but at the end of the day, won't save the world. We desperately need to curb our consumption if we want to be part of the solution and not add to the problems affecting us all – climate change being the most significant.

Smart shopping involves looking for organic, Fairtrade and second-hand or refashioned clothes, and telling high-street retailers, in any way possible, not to niche-market organic/ethical clothes while steering a course to the bottom.

But, overall, the only way to really have a green wardrobe is to buy less and care more. Buying fewer, but better-made clothes may be more expensive but will serve you better in the long term.

And as consumers we can drastically reduce the global climate-change impact of our clothes simply by changing the way we wash and care for them. Washing green means:

- Washing at lower temperatures: 30 °C instead of 40 °C or 60 °C.
- Air drying instead of tumble drying.
- Ironing only if necessary.
- Using eco-friendly washing detergents, with fewer or no phosphates.

Directory

Recommended designers and retailers

Basics

Albatross
Women's pyjamas and lingerie made from organic cotton.
www.albatross-global.com

American Apparel
US-based sweatshop-free enterprise that offers workers unprecedented wages and benefits. Fashion-led and affordable women's wear, men's wear, sportswear, underwear, swimwear, children's clothing, accessories.
www.americanapparel.net

Babygod
Men's fairly traded, organic cotton T-shirts and underwear.
www.babygod.co.uk

Bamboo Clothing
T-shirts, 'activewear' tops, socks for men and women, and men's underwear made from bamboo fabric.
www.bambooclothing.co.uk

Belle and Dean
Animal-print T-shirts, vest tops and baby wear made from organic cotton and screen-printed using water-based ink.
www.belleanddean.com

Bishopston Trading
Women's wear, men's wear, jeans, accessories, children's and baby clothes made using fine handwoven organic cotton and/or an organic cotton calico that is woven on small electric-powered

looms in India. All organic cotton is grown from non-GM seed in India, in the northern state of Gujarat.

www.bishopstontrading.com

Buttress and Snatch

Women's lingerie made in Hackney, London, using real vintage and retro fabrics and trims.

www.buttressandsnatch.co.uk

Calico Moon

Women's wear, men's wear, children's clothing and uniforms, baby clothes, footwear, accessories and jewellery. They have various organic cotton ranges and all suppliers work to Fairtrade guidelines. Their own 'Calico Moon' fair-trade range is made by women who have been rescued from trafficking in Nepal by the Esther Benjamin's Trust.

www.calico-moon.co.uk

Cat's Eye

Organic cotton T-shirts.

www.catseyeworld.com

Chandi Chowk

Specializing in handmade women's wear, men's wear, accessories and jewellery, Chandi Chowk has long-standing fair-trade partnerships with many different groups of crafts people across India and Bangladesh. They also have an organic cotton collection.

www.chandichowk.co.uk

Clothworks

Women's wear (includes a designer collection 'Boutique

Ethique'), children's wear and jewellery. Works with organic cotton, organic linen and hemp, wild and peace silk, and uses natural or AZO-free dyes.
www.boutique-ethique.co.uk

Colonel Kilgore Clothing
T-shirts and surf wear made with organic cotton.
www.colonelkilgoreclothing.com

Conkers Clothing
100 per cent Fairtrade and organic cotton T-shirts and hoodies.
www.conkersclothing.co.uk

E-co Clothing
Women's wear and men's wear made from 100 per cent organic cotton; jeans made from a blend of organic and recycled cotton.
www.e-co-clothing.com

Eczema Clothing
Anti-itch eczema nightwear, cotton gloves and school wear for children; socks, tights, underwear and nightwear for men and women – all made from soft, 100 per cent organic cotton.
www.eczemaclothing.eu

El Alto
Outdoor clothing and equipment company which has a fair-trade partnership with manufacturers in Bolivia.
www.elalto.co.uk

Epona
Blank Fairtrade cotton T-shirts, hoodies and polo tops. Dyes are low impact, AZO-free and heavy metal-free and have been

approved by organic certification bodies. Epona is helping to convert two villages with 150 farmers in Andhra Pradesh, India, to Fairtrade and organic 'in conversion'.

www.eponasport.com

Equop

Fair-trade and organic T-shirts and hoodies. Cotton is sourced from Agrocel, which works with local farmers to produce and process fair-trade organic cotton.

www.equop.com

Ethical Threads

T-shirts made from 100 per cent organic Fairtrade-certified cotton sourced from India.

www.ethicalthreads.co.uk

Fairganic Ltd

T-shirts for men, women and children made from organic cotton grown in Northern India by a farmers' co-operative.

www.fairganic.co.uk

Feral T-shirts

T-shirts made from fairly traded 100 per cent organic cotton. They give 10 per cent of profit to the Climate Group.

www.feralinternational.com

Freedom Clothing Project

Men's wear, women's wear, children's clothing and accessories. Has fair-trade partnerships with organic cotton farms and spinning and textiles factories in Turkey.

http://freedom-clothing.co.uk

Funky Gandhi

T-shirts for men and women made with certified organic cotton. Has long-term fair-trade relationships with suppliers.

www.funkygandhi.com

Gaiam

Yoga and sportswear for women and children, and towelling bathrobes made from organic cotton.

www.gaiamdirect.co.uk

Glow for Life

T-shirts for men, women and children made from 100 per cent organic cotton.

www.glo4life.com

Gossypium

Women's wear, men's wear, sportswear, nightwear, maternity clothes, women's lingerie, children's pyjamas and babygrows. Gossypium has direct contact with every part of their supply chain and has long-term fair-trade partnerships with organic cotton farmers (through sister company Agrocel) and factories in India. They use minimal chemical dyes and finishes (no AZOs or chlorine bleaches, etc.), and use water-based ink for printing.

www.gossypium.co.uk

Greenfibres

Men's wear, women's wear, sportswear, nightwear, bathrobes, underwear, socks and footwear, baby clothes and accessories, and children's clothing. Made from organic fabrics: cotton, linen, silk and hemp. Clothing is also chemical-free (no synthetic chemical finishes or treatments); dyes are derived from plants or minerals, or are environmentally responsible low-

impact dyes. Greenfibres also sell organic fabrics and wool for making your own clothes and furnishings.
www.greenfibres.co.uk

Green Knickers Ltd

Fair-trade and organic knickers made from organic cotton and hemp or specially designed man-made cellulose fibres. Dyes are AZO-free.
www.greenknickers.org

Hebridean Woolhouse

Knitted and woven products made from undyed wool from Hebridean sheep.
www.hebrideanwoolhouse.com

Howies

Women's wear, men's wear, sportswear, jeans, jackets, underwear and accessories. Made from organic cotton and recycled textiles and traceable, sustainable merion fibre. Howies are pioneering their own 'organic denim' and their jeans are eco ball-washed instead of using enzyme or pumice stones. Dyes are natural and low-impact; and Howies minimize the use of chemicals. They give 1 per cent of turnover or 10 per cent of pre-tax profits (whichever is greater) to grass-root environmental and social projects.
www.howies.co.uk

Hug clothing

Women's wear, jeans, baby wear and children's wear made using organic and Fairtrade-certified cotton from Peru.
www.hug.co.uk

Huk Apparel

Fairly traded snow wear made from 100 per cent organic cotton sourced from a farmers' co-operative in India. They give 5 per cent of the revenue from every sale to an 'EthicSnow Fund'.
www.hukapparel.co.uk

Icons Incorporated

They sell 100 per cent organic fair-trade T-shirts dyed using environmentally friendly ink.
www.icons-incorporated.com

Inbi Hemp

Women's wear and men's wear made from 100 per cent hemp and hemp-rich blends.
www.inbi-hemp.co.uk

Intuitive Organics

Fairly traded organic cotton T-shirts screen-printed using water-based dyes.
www.intuitiveorganics.co.uk

Isle of Mull Weavers

Knitwear, organic tweeds, throws, shawls and scarves woven using native undyed Hebridean and Shetland wools. Includes a designer collection. Suits, coats and kilts are made to order.
www.isleofmullweavers.co.uk

Kayon T-shirts

Limited-edition, 100 per cent organic cotton, sweatshop-free T-shirts designed by artists. Available at the Natural Store. Kayon ROA is a design-based charity project.
www.kayondesign.com

Liv UK
Women's wear and women's lingerie made from organic cotton.
www.liv-uk.com

Low and Behold
Organic cotton T-shirts. They donate 5 per cent of net profits to charity.
www.lowandbehold.co.uk

Mongrel Clothing
Organic cotton T-shirts.
www.mongrelclothing.co.uk

Natural Clothing
Underwear, socks, slippers and sleepwear for women, men, children and babies, made from organically grown cotton, merino wool and silk with no chemical treatments. Clothing is either uncoloured (obtains its natural colour from the grown fibre) or, if dyed, only non-AZO, non-heavy metal and low-impact reactive dyes are used.
www.naturalclothing.co.uk

Natural Colour Cotton
Clothing for women, children and babies made either from naturally pigmented cotton fibres or from organic white cotton (dyed using vegetable dyes).
www.naturalcolourcotton.com

The Natural Dye Company
Hand-knitted, naturally dyed jackets, coats and cardigans in silk, wool and cashmere.
www.naturaldyecompany.com

Nature's Mistress

Women's wear made from 'tree cotton' grown in the foothills of the Himalayas, using sustainable perma-culture systems and following ethics of 'earth care, people care and fair share'. The cotton trees grow on terraced edges beside food crops and on land unsuitable for growing food. The trees become established in the local eco-system, and do not require chemical pesticides or fertilizers. Cotton is hand spun into yarn then dyed in small batches using plant-based dyes, and dried in the sun. The yarn is woven using simple traditional wooden looms.

www.naturesmistress.co.uk

One World Is Enough

Women's wear, men's wear, children's wear and accessories sourced from a network of fair-trade suppliers in India, Nepal, Indonesia and Thailand.

www.one-world-is-enough.net

Organic Pure Wool

Hand-knitted clothing from organic wool.

http://organicwoollies.co.uk

Organknickers

Organic cotton yoga wear and knickers.

www.organickers.co.uk

Pachacuti

Fair-trade men's wear, women's wear, children's wear, slippers and accessories created by groups in the Andes using traditional skills. Panama hats are woven by women in two co-operatives which support 400 weavers in the Cuenca region of Ecuador.

www.pachacuti.co.uk

Pakucho
T-shirts made from naturally pigmented, organic fair-trade cotton grown in Peru.
www.pakucho.co.uk

Pardess
Pretty vests and hand-embroidered shoppers made in London. Pardess works with organic cotton, hemp and bamboo, and printing is from Soil Association-approved organic printers. Cleaning practices use only organic and biodegradable products. They give 10 per cent of the profit from every shopper purchased to nature conservation charities.
www.organic-clothes-london.co.uk

Patagonia
Women's wear, men's wear and children's wear including outdoor and active clothing, jackets, hats, footwear and accessories. Ten years ago, Patagonia switched exclusively to organic cotton. They also work with hemp, recycled and recyclable polyester and chlorine-free wool. Their Common Threads Recycling programme makes new garments from old.
www.patagonia.com

Ralper
Organic cotton T-shirts.
www.ralper.co.uk

Rhubarb & Custard
Organic cotton T-shirts, available at the Natural Store.
www.thenaturalstore.co.uk

Seasalt

In 2005 the first fashion brand in the UK to have clothing certified to Soil Association standards, Seasalt's own brand of organic cotton clothing includes women's wear, men's wear and beach towels. Shopping bags are paper carrier bags certified by FSC (Forest Stewardship Council) or bags made from organically grown jute. Committed to ethical trading, where possible Seasalt visit the factories where their garments are produced.

www.seasaltorganic.co.uk

Soliloquy Clothing

Sweatshop-free and charity-endorsed T-shirts, and hoodies made from Fairtrade organic cotton, screen-printed in the UK using environmentally friendly ink.

www.soliloquyclothing.com

SOS Sushi, Save Our Seas Campain

T-shirts featuring designs by British artists such as Tracey Emin. Wholesale profits fund marine conservation programmes.

www.globalocean.eu

Sunrise Screen Print Workshop

Unbleached cotton, organic cotton and hemp T-shirts.

www.menmuir.org.uk

Surfers Against Sewage

SAS first started using organic cottons and environmentally friendly dyes in 2003. In 2007 all their clothes are made with 100 per cent organic cotton, and printed using PVC-free and phthalate-free inks. All purchases of SAS women's wear, men's wear and accessories support SAS campaigns.

http://surfersagainstsewage.co.uk

Terramar Organics

Organic cotton women's wear, men's wear, underwear and children's T-shirts and accessories. Terramar only deal with producers who have ethical labour practices. Where possible, they use local expertise and talent to produce their products, to minimize clothes miles.

www.terramar.co.uk

The Hemp Store

Women's wear, men's wear and T-shirts made from a blend of hemp and organic cotton; scarves, rucksacks and canvas sneakers made from hemp and cotton; and shawls made from Himalayan nettle fibre.

www.thehempstore.co.uk

The White T-shirt Company

T-shirts made from 'green cotton' which is monitored from germination to production for its environmental impact.

www.thewhitetshirt.co.uk

THTC

Fairly traded T-shirts and hoodies made from organically grown hemp and organic cotton. Also use recycled PET, Tencel and other eco fibres. THTC uses water-based inks with a discharge screen-printing process for almost all new designs. Clothing is made in ethically audited factories in eastern China where employment standards have been implemented and are rigorously checked.

www.thtc.co.uk

Third Transition

Ethically sourced T-shirts printed using water-based ink; they also have an organic cotton range.

www.thirdtransition.com

Timberland

Women's wear, men's wear, footwear and accessories. Timberland work with organic cotton, recycled cotton, hemp, recycled fleece, bamboo and Vibram Ecostep (using the scraps left over from cut-out soles).

Their environmentally friendly packaging and 'Our Footprint' product labelling provide details about the environmental and community impact, and they use renewable energy sources (solar, wind, water) at some of their factories and distribution centres. The flagship Timberland store in London is furnished with reclaimed floorboards, Victorian doors and beams sourced from a variety of demolished schools and churches around the country. Other fixtures have been designed using sustainably sourced oak and beech, and sustainably farmed cork, hessian and bamboo, and all paints are water-based.

www.timberlandbootcompany.co.uk

Tonic T-shirts

Organic and fairly traded T-shirts and hoodies.

www.tonictshirts.co.uk

Traidcraft

'The UK's leading fair-trade organization' sells women's wear, men's wear, nightwear, shoes, accessories and jewellery. Products are sourced from more than 100 producer groups in over 30 countries.

www.traidcraftshop.co.uk

Zoozoo 2

They sell 100 per cent organic cotton T-shirts and fair-trade jewellery.

www.zoozoo2.com

Designer wear

Alchem1st

Fairly traded women's wear made in Bali (in spacious open-air factories set in tropical gardens), designed and created by local crafts people who specialize in hand embroidery and intricate jewellery. A percentage of profits is donated to a local Balinese orphanage to provide children with books, teachers, clothes, etc.

www.alchem1st.com

Amana

Chic women's wear handmade from organic cotton, hemp and silk mixes, chunky hemp cord and hemp denim. Future collections may include Tencel, flax, bamboo, recycled fabrics, organic and wild silks, and organic wool. Only natural or AZO-free dyes are used. Amana have a long-term fair-trade partnership with women artisans in a Moroccan village.

www.amana-collection.com

Amira

Fairly traded one-off and limited-edition delicate drawstring minidresses and blouses made using end-of-run and certified organic fabrics. Amira work in participation with small-scale producers in India.

www.amirawear.com

Anatomy

Stylish women's wear made from natural and organic fabrics such as hemp, cotton, linen, Tencel and peace silk from sustainable and ethical sources. Where dyes are used they are natural or low-impact.

www.anatomyfashion.co.uk

Bamford and Sons

Men's wear, including T-shirts, muslin shirts, canvas trousers and chinos, denim jeans and jackets, made using 100 per cent organic cotton; accessories made with chemical-free leathers; and hemp bags.

www.bamfordandsons.com

Ciel

Hip and luxurious women's wear, lingerie and accessories. Ciel use a wide range of certified organic cottons, linens, bamboo and hemp/silk blends along with Oeko-Tex 100-certified fabrics and recycled post-manufactured textile industrial waste. Dyes are AZO-free. There's a 'future heirloom' range of timeless modern designs that can be built on each season and garments come with guidelines on using low wash temperatures. One of the first UK fashion companies to be carbon neutral, Ciel have a partnership with the Save the Amazon Rainforest Organization (STARO).

www.ciel.ltd.uk

Davina Hawthorne

Cutting-edge clothes for women, handcrafted in the UK. Fabrics are recycled, manipulated embroidered and printed, and often sculptural, using handcrafted and industrial processes.

www.davinahawthorne.com

Debbi Little

Bespoke dresses made from recycled 1945 parachutes, dyed using natural dyes.

www.equaclothing.com

Del Forte

Eco luxury line of women's denim clothing crafted from 100 per cent organic cotton grown in California and Texas and sewn and finished in Los Angeles, a city that is leading the way in anti-sweatshop legislation and enforcement, and is home to the most cutting-edge wash development facilities in the country.

The Del Forte Denim Outreach Program, in partnership with the Sustainable Cotton Project, aims to create relationships with and provide resources for the agricultural workers who help make their clothing. The Rejeaneration project offers to take back Del Forte jeans at the end of their consumer life and use them to make patches or to be refashioned into other garments.

www.delforte.com

Denise Bird Woven Textiles

Work with eco fibres – mostly natural and woven in their naturally coloured, undyed state, although natural dye pigments are occasionally applied. Fibres include organic cotton, UK-reared alpaca, hemp, bamboo, silk noil, fibre from recycled plastic bottles, Tencel and soybean fibre. Fibres are often from fairly traded sources.

www.denisebirdwoventextiles.com

Edun

Edun is a full fashion collection for men and women, including tops, bottoms, denim, dresses, jackets, knits and sweaters, accessories and jewellery. Edun's mission is to create beautiful clothing, while fostering sustainable employment in developing areas of the world, in particular Africa. They are working towards using more organic materials in the collection. In 2007, Edun launched the edun LIVE brand. They aim to help foster trade in Africa through high-volume sales of blank T-shirts to the wholesale market. From the fields where the cotton is picked, to the final printing process, all edun LIVE products are 100 per cent African. *www.edunonline.com*

Emmeline 4 Re
Emmeline 4 Re work with recycled textiles, transforming offcuts, ripped or end-of-roll fabric remnants into funky women's clothing. Fabrics and linings are sourced from textile manufacturers and the Salvation Army Trading Company Ltd; buttons, threads and zips are donated from various sources: companies, people interested in recycling, friends and family.
www.emmeline4re.co.uk

Enamore
A creative fashion label that make flirty, feminine women's clothing, lingerie and accessories. The collection is produced from hemp, cotton and peace silk fabrics, and from vintage prints and reclaimed fabrics. Made in the UK at the Enamore studio in Bath, by outworkers in their own homes or studios, and by a small production unit in London. Everything possible from the studio is recycled, including fabric offcuts, which are either reused or donated to schools' art departments.
www.enamore.co.uk

Eternal Creation
Women's dresses, camisoles, kimonos, wraps, pyjamas and

slippers, and clothing for children and babies, crafted and ethically produced in Dharamsala, a Tibetan refugee community in northern India, where a particular focus is women's employment and training.
www.eternalcreation.com

Fisher Garcia
Handcrafted fashion designed to be timeless. Decorative details include felting, cutwork, embroidery and shibori dyeing. Fabrics are organic and fair trade whenever available and dyes are metal-free and contain no banned amines.
www.fishergarcia.com

Frank & Faith
Fashionable, ethically made women's wear from organic, recycled or sustainable yarns and fabrics. Frank & Faith manufacture in Britain, supporting and nurturing small factories and businesses often in areas of deprived communities with high unemployment.
www.frankandfaith.com

From Somewhere
Recycle 'fashion waste' – from production cuts to fabric colour charts – of famous fabric manufacturers, to create funky, fresh designs mixing cashmere, silk, cotton, jersey and tweed. Made with fair labour in the EU.
www.fromsomewhere.co.uk

Gary Harvey
A range of couture-inspired dresses made entirely from recycled garments. All the dresses are made to order.
www.garyharveycreative.com

Goodone

Women's wear, men's wear and accessories sourced from textile recycling factories in London. You can co-design your own piece by providing material.

www.goodone.co.uk

Ivana Cavallo

Knitwear handmade in England from natural yarns, available from the Natural Store.

www.thenaturalstore.co.uk

Izzy Lane

Knitwear for men and women using the wool from sheep rescued from certain slaughter for being male, for missing a pregnancy, for being a little lame, too small or too old, or for having 'imperfections' such as a black spot in a white fleece. Wool is spun, dyed and weaved or knitted in the UK.

www.izzylane.co.uk

Jo Pott Mercer

Clothes for women made using ancient techniques like block printing, weaving and appliqué – making traditional skills marketable. Jo Pott has fair-trade partnerships with village-based producers in India and Nepal.

www.jopott.com

Junky Styling

Deconstructed second-hand clothing reworked into unique garments. Their signature men's and women's line is produced in their shop in East London from recycled suits, coats and wools. They believe in fair labour; recycle as much waste as possible and, if using new fabrics, endeavour for them to be organic.

www.junkystyling.co.uk

Katharine Hamnett

The Katharine E. Hamnett (E is for ethical and environmental) range of clothes for men and women is 'unqualifiedly' ethical – all the cotton is organic and made under fair labour conditions. Many items are produced in the UK, supporting artisanal leather making, weaving, spinning and knitting.

www.katharinehamnett.com

Keep and Share

Knitwear hand-knitted in the UK.

www.keepandshare.co.uk

Makepiece

Designer knitwear company with ethics: real fashion, not passing fads; using natural sustainable fibres; sourcing as locally as possible (Beate Kubitz, its founder, even keeps her own sheep); using undyed and natural dyed yarns; ensuring fair labour and high animal welfare. Made in the UK.

www.makepiece.co.uk

MUMO

Focus on developing established fashion labels into being fair-trade products, bringing talent from developing countries to the UK. A proportion of revenue made here is reinvested down the supply chain to improve the lives of the communities where the clothes are actually made. MUMO represent three women's wear labels from Brazil: Zigfreda, Huis Clos and Kylza Ribas.

www.mumo-uk.com

Noir

Tailored and luxurious fair-trade fashion. Noir has created its own cotton fabric brand, Illuminati II, made from raw ingredients sourced from Uganda. Illuminati II's vision is to deliver organic and Fair-trade cotton fabrics while ensuring sustainability of the Humane Business Model from the heart of Africa.

www.illuminati2-noir.com

People Tree

Fair-trade and ecological clothing and accessories for women, men, children and babies. People Tree pay producers fair prices, making advance payments when needed, and they promote traditional skills and rural development. Their organic cotton farmers in India receive a 30 per cent premium above conventional cotton prices – and they commit to buying the cotton before the crop is grown. Clothing is dyed using low-impact, AZO-free dyes. They use locally available and natural materials where possible, including handmade recycled paper products, products made from jute and other environmentally friendly materials.

www.ptree.co.uk

Pierre Garroudi

One-off, unique designs made from found or donated materials. He also makes to order – provide your own material and he can create a shirt, dress or a bag – whatever you want.

www.pierregarroudi.com

Red Mutha

Colourful one-off, customized, recycled garments for men and women 'who dare to wear them'. They have a bespoke customization service – email your requests and send in an item. *www.redmutha.com*

Rianne de Witte

Work with eco fabrics: Lyocell (wood pulp), PLA (Polylactide) made from corn, organic certified cotton, linen, and with natural vegetable dyes such as meekrap, a root which gives a red colour. Traceability and fair labour is ensured by the 'MADE BY' label (*www.made-by.org*), an umbrella label used by fashion brands and retailers to show consumers that their clothes are produced in a sustainable manner.
www.riannedewitte.nl

Sari

Women's wear collection made exclusively from recycled saris collected by the Save a Sari Campaign. Each garment is unique. Sari donate 10 per cent of their sales to a children's charity.
www.saricouture.com

Snood

Knitwear for men, women and babies, handmade from reclaimed and vintage wool. Sourced, designed and made in the UK.
www.snood-revolution.co.uk

Stewart & Brown

Functional and fashionable women's wear collection comprised of five product categories. ORGNC: organic cotton-knit fabrics made in Los Angeles under the Californian labour codes. CSHMR: Mongolian cashmere produced and knitted by indigenous people in Mongolia to support and sustain their centuries-old way of life. KNITS: premium knitwear made with all-natural fibres. SURP+: made from excess material and fabrics. GREEN: made from fibres cultivated naturally, such as hemp and linen. The SURP+ and GREEN lines are manufactured in Hong Kong and Asia in well-monitored facilities that work with other sustainable and labour-conscious brands.

www.stewartbrown.com

Tam and Rob

Quirky and fashionable women's wear and accessories made from organic and fair-trade cotton and put together by workers in India and Nepal, who earn a fair wage and are treated well. Factories have been accredited by independent third parties through IFAT, the international Fairtrade body, and are inspected by Tam and Rob themselves. Many of their suppliers employ people who would ordinarily be overlooked in the Indian and Nepalese job markets (such as abused women).

www.tamandrob.co.uk

Think! Clothing

Fairly traded stylish women's wear that helps provide India's rural and urban poor with a means of income earned through traditional handloom weaving and garment production. Fabric dyes are AZO-free.

www.thinkfairtrade.com

TRAIDremade

Recycled-fashion label TRAIDremade follows the fashion trends widely available on the high street. TRAIDremade designers give torn and stained clothing a new lease of life by mixing, matching, ripping, cutting, sewing and printing. They work exclusively with donated materials, and each and every piece is completely one-off and original.

www.traid.org.uk/remade.html

Truly Sopel

Beach boob tubes, garden dresses, tops, tunics, circular skirts, macs, capes, coats and belts made in London from vintage fabrics.

www.trulysopel.co.uk

Unicorn

'Feminine and fun' women's wear made from natural eco-dyed fabrics: organic cotton, wool, linen, wild silk, hemp and bamboo. Fabrics are as fairly sourced as possible and are made in Ireland by a group of traveller women in Wicklow as part of a government-sponsored scheme helping them to stay in employment and develop their skills. They have a Shakti Yoga/living wear label that uses organic cotton.

www.unicorndesign.net

Wildlife Works

Fashion-led women's T-shirts, jersey skirts, shirts, stylish trousers and pretty dresses made in an eco-friendly factory in Kenya next to a 32,000 hectare Wildlife Sanctuary (both created and operated by Wildlife Works). The factory employs local people to create the garments using organic cotton and other environmentally friendly fibres. For every person employed making clothes, they employ one person in land and animal conservation. Wildlife Works have also built four schools and support the education of 1,200 local schoolchildren. Proceeds of product sales go towards saving endangered and threatened wildlife around the globe.

www.wildlifeworks.co.uk

Internet eco boutiques that stock designer wear

Adili

Quentin Griffiths, Christopher Powles and Adam Smith launched the Adili website in September 2006. 'We saw a unique opportunity, in terms of a growing consumer interest for organic and fair-trade products, to create a fashion business with ethics at the core,' says Adam. They currently stock 47 brands – including women's wear, men's wear and baby clothes – and aim to expand this to 60–70 later this year. 'There is also a list in our office of over 200 brands that we would love to work with and some of which we are in discussions with,' says Adam. Five per cent of the company's share capital has been allocated to fund a foundation to independently further environmental and social justice objectives in the garment industry, which they aim to launch in late 2007.

www.adili.com

DeviDoll

DeviDoll started trading in September 2007. DeviDoll was Sindhu Venkatanarayanan's answer to the dilemma of reconciling 'high-end fashion taste with a desire to purchase fashion that is (at the very least) less "dirty" than most fashion today'. Every label at DeviDoll has to meet at least one of the following: made from organic fabric or alternative fabric (for example hemp, bamboo, peace silk); benefits children and/or women in its production; revives ancient handicrafts among local populations; made from vintage or reused materials. Designers across a full range of clothing are 'fused with' strong aesthetic sensibility and awareness of international trends in the fashion world.

'DeviDoll aims to be more than just a boutique – the idea is to be an incubator for a particular type of designer, like an eco-

Browns, if you will. By choosing the designers we do and promoting them, I hope to further populate the eco-fashion space (a good thing in itself) and also to support, via these environmentally and socially minded designers and their work, various ethical causes that are important,' Sindhu says.
www.devidoll.com

Ecobtq

Ecobtq was launched in Hove, East Sussex in June 2006. 'My decision to do this was based around my personal struggle to find places to buy special eco-friendly items that were also fashionable,' says Madeleine King. Suppliers and designers are found through word of mouth, contacts within the industry, attending eco fairs and launches, reading the press and researching on the internet. Ecobtq are looking to expand their current product offer by adding men's and children's categories, and will be developing exclusive 'ecobtq' products with their designers.
www.ecobtq.com

Equa Clothing

Starting business in 2005 in Islington's Camden Passage, as London's first all organic and fair-trade clothing store, Equa Clothing have gone from stocking nine different designer labels to 24 today. They went online in October 2006. Founder Penny Cooke says that finding new labels isn't difficult: 'We are contacted by new labels that have set up or are setting up new fair-trade labels, or we research the industry ourselves online or by attending events put on by the ethical fashion industry.'
www.equaclothing.com

The Natural Store

Ismat Osman and Rachel Rogers founded the Natural Store over 18 months ago as a 'one-stop shop for stylish and unique high-quality organic and ethical goods'. Products range from fashion to interiors, beauty to food, baby wear to travel. 'With over 50 ethical fashion brands for men and ladies, from cottage industry designers just starting out with their label to larger more established brands, the number of brands on the Natural Store is growing all the time, which makes us – we believe – the largest UK ethical retailer online for the number of different brands and collections available,' says Rachel.

www.thenaturalstore.co.uk

Jeans

Ascension Clothing

www.ascensionclothing.co.uk

Del Forte

www.delforte.com

Edun

www.edunonline.com

Greenfibres

www.greenfibres.co.uk

Hennes

www.hm.com

Howies

www.howies.co.uk

Hug
www.hug.co.uk

James Jeans
www.jamesjeans.us

Kuyichi
www.kuyichi.com

Levis
www.levistrauss.com

Loomstate
www.loomstate.org

Mavi
www.mavi.com

Replay Jeans
www.replaybluejeans.com

Serfontaine
www.serfontaine.com

Shoes

Beyond Skin
Ethical women's shoes – handmade, vegetarian and sexy, including high heels, stilettos, pumps and flats.
www.beyondskin.co.uk

Birkenstock
Range includes vegetable-tanned and vegan shoes. They aim to

reduce the energy consumption of machinery and heating equipment.

www.birkenstock.co.uk

Black Spot Shoes

Black Spot make hard-wearing boots that have organic-hemp uppers, recycled car-tyre soles and vegetarian toes, and organic-hemp sneakers with rubber soles and toe caps that are 70 per cent biodegradable. Shoes are made in a safe, comfortable, unionized factories with environmentally sound practices. Black Spot shoes are a project of the Adbusters Media Foundation.

http://adbusters.org/metas/corpo/blackspotshoes/

Charmoné Shoes

Beautiful, luxurious shoes fairly made in Italy from animal-free, eco-friendly materials. They give 5 per cent of all profits to charities that support people, animals and the environment.

www.charmoneshoes.com

Green Shoes

Shoes, boots, sandals and leather accessories for men, women and children, handmade in Devon from leather or vegan material. Leather is processed using vegetable tannins, and is undyed. Materials are sourced from UK suppliers.

www.greenshoes.co.uk

Fair Deal Trading

Fairly traded trainers made with sustainably tapped natural rubber. A fair-trade premium is paid for each pair produced.

www.fairdealtrading.com

Freerangers
Vegan shoes and accessories.
www.freerangers.co.uk

Hetty Rose 'Imari' Vintage Kimono Shoes
All Hetty Rose shoes are made to order, taking from five to eight weeks to cut, stitch and make, and can be made in the size and material of your choice from a selection of exquisite vintage Japanese kimono fabrics.
www.thenaturalstore.co.uk

Jinga
Ethically produced trainers from Brazil made using no animal products. A percentage of profits (5 per cent minimum) helps fund a social project in a Rio de Janeiro favela.
www.jingashop.com

Last Footwear
Handcrafted shoes made with vegetable-tanned leather. Glues used are water-based.
www.lastfootwear.com

Meher Kakalia
Hand-stitched leather slippers.
www.meherkakalia.com

New Balance Trainers
Trainers made in the UK.
www.newbalance.co.uk

Po-Zu 'Hiraku' Slippers
Made in Glastonbury, England, Po-Zu use pure natural materials

that are as near as possible to their natural state, with the least amount of processing. All materials are biodegradable and free from harmful chemicals and, if possible, organic. The upper is made from organically tanned woven leather, unlined, and the foot-mattress bedding is organically tanned suede. Both leathers are tanned with vegetable extracts from the bark of Mimosa and Quebracho trees. The foot-mattress filler is 60 per cent coconut husk and 40 per cent natural latex. The sole is made from 100 per cent natural latex (pure vegetable rubber made from the milky sap of the Lectae Hevea tree). Po-Zu avoid harmful glues by stitching their shoes together, also making them more breathable, durable, repairable and recyclable.

www.thenaturalstore.co.uk

Recycle Your Jeans
Take in old blue jeans and transform them into Denim Kalahari sandals. The parent company of Recycle Your Jeans is Softwalker Ltd, one of a very small handful of shoemaking companies still manufacturing in the UK. The Kalahari sandal is an ultra-comfortable, soft, springy sandal, which can help 'improve general posture and foot health'. The sandals have a unique foot support that mimics walking barefoot on soft ground.

www.recycleyourjeans.com/

Simple Shoes
Made from natural materials: jute, cork, bamboo, natural crepe rubber, and wool felt.

www.thenaturalstore.co.uk

Stella McCartney
Shoes and bags that are 100 per cent vegetarian.

www.stellamccartney.com

Terra Plana

Shoes are made from eco-friendly materials including chrome-free leathers, vegetable-tanned leathers, recycled materials, pure latex soling materials, recycled rubber soles, recycled foam foot beds and E-Leather, a leather by-product made from a blend of leather and textile fibres. The E-Leather is produced with closed-loop water usage and best-practice pollution prevention methods. The Terra Plana range includes Worn Again, trainers made with recycled materials from prison blankets, car seats, E-Leather and reclaimed jeans; and Vivo Barefoot, shoes that feature an ultra-thin puncture-resistant sole giving the wearer all the benefits of walking barefoot.
www.terraplana.com

The Natural Shoe Store
www.thenaturalshoestore.com

The Wet Felting Company

Slippers made from locally sourced chemical-free fleeces that can be repaired or resoled.
www.wetfeltingcompany.co.uk

Vegetarian Shoes
www.vegetarian-shoes.co.uk

Accessories
Again NYC

Limited-edition handbags, purses and yoga mat bags made from vintage, rescued and repurposed materials and fabrics.
www.againnyc.com

AmazonLife

Shoppers, shoulder bags and clutch bags handmade from sustainably sourced wild organic rubber by the rubber-tapping tribal communities of the Amazon Basin, who depend on rubber-tapping activity to survive in the forest. AmazonLife, in alliance with Rubber Tappers Associations, has developed Treetap sustainable production, helping to protect over 900,000 hectares of wild forest from exploitation.

www.amazonlife.com.br/store/

Art Works for Africa

Shopper basket bags and beaded jewellery sourced directly from designers and craftspeople in Africa. The aim is to promote sustainable business in Africa by developing long-term relationships with suppliers, sourcing products on an ethical basis, and assisting in developing design and business skills.

www.artworksforafrica.com

Cebra

Fair-trade accessories include ethically sound handbags designed and handmade from sustainable sources in Kenya, Madagascar, Nepal, Brazil and Peru; and wild silk shawls handwoven and naturally dyed by a co-op in Madagascar. They also have a range of fair-trade jewellery.

www.cebraonline.com

Doy Bags

A range of bags, purses and accessories made from recycled juice packs – packaging that would otherwise go into landfill sites and incinerators. Doy Bags are produced and traded according to fair-trade principles.

www.thenaturalstore.co.uk

Entermodal

Sustainably produced leather bags made from vegetable-tanned leather free from formaldehyde and heavy metals. Each bag is designed for ease of deconstruction to facilitate the recycling of the leather and the other materials for future products.

www.entermodal.com

Flamma Design

Stylish range of bags handmade from vegetable-tanned leather. Nothing artificial has been used in their production.

www.flammadesign.co.uk

Freeset

Fair trade jute bags.

www.freesetbags.com

Ganesha

A fair-trade shop selling bags and accessories sourced from co-operatives and producer associations in developing countries, and from indigenous groups and small-scale producers concentrating on traditional materials and industries. Most of their producers are members of IFAT (International Federation for Alternative Trade).

www.ganesha.co.uk

Hatti Trading

Hatti Trading sell ladies', men's and children's bags, and have fair-trade partnerships with women's groups in Nepal.

www.hattitrading.co.uk

Helen Riegle Designs

Bags made from hemp canvas, animal-friendly ultrasuede and

sustainably produced Treetap wild rubber from the Amazon.

www.thenaturalstore.co.uk

Hini

Pretty bags made from salvaged and recycled faux leather (which is then appliquéd and embroidered).

www.hiniboutique.com

Jiva Fair Trading

Fairly traded bags, scarves and jewellery.

www.jivafairtrading.com

Just Bazaar

Contemporary fair-trade goods including shoulder bags made from water buffalo leather, butterfly-shaped felt bags and necklaces handmade in Peru from choloque seeds.

www.justbazaar.co.uk

La Vie Devant Soie

Fairly traded fashionable accessories (bags, clutch bags, hats, scarves, etc.) made by artisans in Cambodia.

www.adili.com/brands/la_vie_devant_soie.html

Maria

Innovative, funky bags made from original fabrics from the 1960s and 1970s, recycled garments and eco fur.

www.supra-maria.com

Martha Evatt

One-off bags made of vintage kimonos.

www.thenaturalstore.co.uk

Matt & Nat

Canadian-based Matt & Nat produce a 'fashion-forward line of vegan handbags' as well as wallets and other accessories in a range of styles and colours. They use PU as well as polyvinyl chloride (PVC).

www.mattandnat.com

Nahui Ollin

Colourful handbags made in Mexico from recycled sweet wrappers and fizzy-drink labels. All materials come from misprint and surplus production at factories in central Mexico. Nahui Ollin have set up a cottage industry that currently employs more than 400 craftsmen. They provide training and create consistent, well-paid jobs in communities where there are many unemployed artisans.

www.nahuiollin.com

Onelessplasticbag

Pretty fabric shopper bags made from organic or recycled materials. Strong yet light, they can fold into a small pocket that goes easily into the smallest of handbags.

www.oneless.krata.co.uk

Onya Bags

Made of parachute material, Onya Bags are light and yet strong and highly durable; and they are packed in a little pouch, so can fit into a handbag. They also come in a huge range of colours.

www.onyabags.co.uk

Organic Wool Company

Scarves and shawls manufactured in Wales using wool from organic sheep and from sheep in conversion to organic status.

Processed without the use of harmful chemicals.
www.organicwool.co.uk

Posch
Pretty shopper bags made from vintage fabric.
www.thenaturalstore.co.uk

Refab
Bags made from classic vintage fabrics and other reclaimed, recycled, organic and biodegradable materials.
www.refab.co.uk

Smart Tart
Handmade designer handbags in antique and recycled fabrics.
www.smarttart.co.uk

Suitcase London
Bags made from recycled suit jackets.
www.suitcase-london.com

Tree 2 My Door
Eco-friendly shopper bags made from jute.
www.tree2mydoor.com

Use UK
Unique bags handcrafted from 100 per cent leather remnants (a by-product of the furniture industry) and a vintage buckle.
www.use-uk.com

Voodooblue
Basket bags handwoven at a women's co-operative in Kenya.
www.voodooblue.co.uk

Jewellery

Cred Jewellery

Guilt-free gold wedding rings, diamond engagement rings and bespoke jewellery. Cred has fair-trade partnerships with small-scale mining communities (Oro Verde), cutting and polishing co-operative workshops, master jewellers and stone setters. Their strict environmental policy ensures that 'no toxic chemicals are used during the mining process'; 'topsoil removed from the mined area should be saved and replaced at the end of the extraction procedure'; and 'the mined area should gain ecological stability within three years'.

www.cred.tv

Fifi Bijoux

A luxury ethical jewellery company that creates pendants, rings, bracelets and earrings. Gold and gemstones are mined from community-owned, co-operative mines operating eco-sustainability programmes and fair-trade protocols. No chemicals are used in extraction or refining and the land is regenerated after three years.

www.fifibijoux.com

Jungleberry

Fair-trade jewellery made from natural seeds, berries and woods sustainably harvested in the Amazon rainforest.

www.jungleberry.co.uk

made

Fair-trade jewellery and accessories made from sustainable local resources. Designed in England by influential designers such as Pippa Small, made products are then sourced and created in developing countries in Africa and Asia.

www.made.uk.com

Manumit UK

Fair-trade jewellery and accessories, including bags, belts and scarves.

www.manumituk.com

Namaste

Fairly traded jewellery and accessories. In developing markets, such as Nepal, Indonesia and Thailand, they buy only from primary producers. Where necessary, Namaste make advance payments for materials, workers and whatever else is necessary.

www.namaste-uk.com

Silver Chilli

Fair-trade silver jewellery made in Mexico. Silverchilli pay its producers 50 per cent in advance for all the orders to help fund raw materials, and they return 95 per cent of profits back to the community. Each year they invest part or all of their profit in a social project chosen by one of the groups they work with.

www.silverchilli.com

Babies and children

Aravore

www.aravore-babies.com

Baby O

www.baby-o.co.uk

Baby Organics

www.babyorganics.co.uk

Beaming Baby

www.beamingbaby.co.uk

Bella Natura
www.bellanatura.co.uk

BORN
www.borndirect.com

Clean Slate Clothing
Fair-trade school uniforms.
www.cleanslateclothing.co.uk

Clothworks
www.clothworks.co.uk

Cut4Cloth
www.cut4cloth.co.uk

Eco baby basics
www.ecobabybasics.com

Ecobaby
www.ecobaby.com

Global kids
www.globalkids.com

Green Baby
www.greenbaby.co.uk

Greensleeves
www.greensleevesclothing.com

Hejhog
www.hejhog.co.uk

Huggababy
www.huggababy.co.uk

Kitty Kins
www.kittykins.co.uk

Little Green Earthlets
www.earthlets.com

Mini Organic
www.mini-organic.co.uk

Natural Nursery
www.naturalnursery.co.uk

Nature's Fibres
www.naturesfibres.com

Organics for Kids
www.organicsforkids.co.uk

Smile Child
www.smilechild.co.uk

Tatty Bumpkin
www.tattybumpkin.com

Fabrics of the future

E-Leather

www.eleatherltd.com

Isle of Mull Weavers

www.ardalanishfarm.co.uk

Natural Dyes

www.gracieburnett.com

Sustainable Cotton Project

www.sustainablecotton.org

DIY fashion

Second-hand
Oxfam

www.oxfam.org.uk/shop/index.htm

TRAID

www.traid.org.uk

Vintage
Anita's Vintage Fashion Fairs

www.vintagefashionfairs.com

Sewing/knitting
www.ukhandknitting.com
www.knitchics.co.uk
www.knitty.com
www.magknits.co.uk

www.loop.gb.com
www.iknit.org.uk

Swapping
Swap-a-Rama Razzmatazz
Parties such as Swap-a-Rama Razzmatazz, founded by Eloise
Markwell-Butler, now a regular event at east London restaurant
Favela Chic. *www.myspace.com/swaparamarazzmatazz*

What's mine is yours
Online portal set up by stylist Judy Berger, which allows its
thousands of members to swap clothes and furniture.
www.whatsmineisyours.com

See also

To find a fair-trade shop near you:
British Association for Fair Trade Shops (BAFTS)
www.bafts.org.uk

To find organic cotton clothing near you:
PAN's 'Wear Organic'
www.wearorganic.org

Campaigning groups
ActionAid
Large global anti-poverty agency that aims to tackle the unfair
rules that govern international trade, and to ensure that the
World Trade Organization works for poor and marginalized
communities. ActionAid's Trade Justice Campaign work in 20
countries across the globe to persuade governments and interna-

tional organizations that current trade rules are unfair. In the UK they put pressure on the government and EU calling on them to ensure that poor countries have the right to choose the best policies, empower women and protect the environment.
www.actionaid.org.uk

Christian Aid
Christian Aid work with the world's poorest people in nearly 50 countries and tackle the causes and consequences of poverty and injustice. Their main campaign is Trade Justice.
www.christian-aid.org.uk

Clean Clothes Campaign (CCC)
International campaign focused on improving working conditions in the global garment and sportswear industries and empowering the workers in it. CCC put pressure on companies to take responsibility to ensure that their garments are produced in decent working conditions; they support workers, trade unions and NGOs in producer countries; they explore legal possibilities for improving working conditions; and they raise awareness among consumers.
www.cleanclothes.org

Environmental Justice Foundation (EJF)
EJF lead an international campaign to resolve the human rights and environmental abuses linked to global cotton production. EJF campaign to raise public awareness of the conditions under which cotton is produced and to press retailers to ensure they only sell 'clean cotton'. They also campaign for an EU regulation on forced child labour, and for cotton products to show the cotton's country of origin on the label.
www.ejfoundation.org

Labour Behind the Label

The UK platform of the international Clean Clothes Campaign supporting garment workers' efforts worldwide to improve their working conditions. LBL educate consumers, lobby companies and government, raise awareness and encourage international solidarity with workers. Members include trade unions, consumer organizations, campaign groups and charities.
www.labourbehindthelabel.org

No Sweat

Campaign against sweatshops and child labour, in the UK and around the world.
www.nosweat.org.uk

Oxfam

Oxfam International is a confederation of 13 organizations working together with over 3,000 partners in more than 100 countries to find lasting solutions to poverty, suffering and injustice. Oxfam work with organizations around the world to shift global trade rules so they start to work for poor people and communities as well as rich. Oxfam's Make Trade Fair campaign is calling on governments, institutions and multinational companies to change the rules so that trade can become part of the solution to poverty, not part of the problem.
www.oxfam.org

People and Planet

The largest, student network in Britain campaigning to alleviate world poverty, defend human rights and protect the environment. There are People and Planet groups at over 55 UK universities that campaign and raise awareness about the global issues by having speakers, debates, quizzes, colourful demonstrations, boycotts, club nights.

www.peopleandplanet.org

Pesticide Action Network (PAN)

A network of over 600 participating non-governmental organizations, institutions and individuals in over 90 countries, working to replace the use of hazardous pesticides with ecologically sound alternatives. PAN projects tackle the problems in different ways: by clearing up the toxic dumps of obsolete pesticides found throughout Africa; by working for a ban of the identified pesticide endosulfan, which is causing death and poisonings; and by helping farmers convert to organic cotton. PAN UK's Wear Organic project aims to raise awareness of organic cotton as benefiting the environment, the livelihoods and the health of poor farmers in developing countries; to ensure information is available to consumers, businesses, fashion colleges, environment and development NGOs, and civil society groups to stimulate demand for more sustainable cotton production and to help increase the market for organic cotton.

www.pan-uk.org

Soil Association

The UK's leading campaigning and certification organization for organic food and farming. SA Certification is the UK's largest organic certification body, established in 1973 – the SA now certify 80 per cent of all organic products sold in the UK. The Soil Association textiles standards were developed over three years up to their launch in 2003. They cover wool, hemp, linen, cotton, flax, skins and leather products and provide the most comprehensive organic standards in the world for these types of products.

www.soilassociation.org

Tear Fund

A leading relief and development charity, working in partnership with Christian agencies and churches worldwide to tackle the causes and effects of global poverty. Tearfund's trade campaign focuses on the responsibility we have as consumers to bring about positive change. Tearfund have a Lift the Label on Fashion campaign and work in partnership with Labour Behind the Label (LBL).

www.tearfund.org

Trade Justice Movement

The Trade Justice Movement is a coalition of more than 80 member organizations including trade unions, aid agencies, environment and human rights campaigns, Fairtrade organizations, faith and consumer groups. TJM campaigns for trade justice – not free trade – with the rules weighted to benefit poor people and the environment.

www.tjm.org.uk

War on Want

Campaigns for workers' rights and against the root causes of global poverty, inequality and injustice. Trade Justice: campaigning for trade rules that put people and the environment before the interests of big business. Corporate Accountability: campaigning for a legally binding set of rules to hold big business to account for its impacts on people and the environment.

www.waronwant.org

Notes

Chapter 1

1. *It's Vintage, Darling! How To Be a Clothes Connoisseur* by Christa Weil, Hodder & Stoughton, Kent, 2006, p.47.
2. *50 Reasons to Buy Fair Trade* by Miles Litvinoff and John Madeley, Pluto Press, London, 2007, p.123.
3. *Well Dressed? The present and future sustainability of clothing and textiles in the United Kingdom,* Institute for Manufacturing (IFM), University of Cambridge, 2006, p.10.
4. ibid. p.10.
5. ibid. p.10.
6. 'Squaring up to Burberry' by Carole Cadwalladr, *Observer Magazine,* 25 March 2007.
7. Quote from Birmingham University's Tom Sorrell, *Observer Magazine,* 25 March 2007.
8. 'Looking for a Quick Fix: How weak social auditing is keeping workers in sweatshops', Clean Clothes Campaign, 2005, p.79.
9. 'Trading Away Our Rights: Women Working in Global Supply Chains', *Oxfam International,* February 2004.
10. Briefing on the Chinese Garment Industry, Ruth Domoney, Labour Behind the Label, February 2007.
11. ibid.
12. ibid.
13. Quoted in 'Check out cut-price £3 jeans', *Bristol Evening Post,* 2 April 2005.
14. 'Who Pays? How British Supermarkets are Keeping Women

Workers in Poverty', ActionAid, 2007, p.14.

15. ibid. p.15.
16. 'Who Pays for Cheap Clothes? 5 Questions the low-cost retailers must answer', Labour Behind the Label, July 2006, p.7.
17. ibid. p.11.
18. ibid. p.11.
19. 'Who Pays?', ActionAid, p.16.
20. ibid. p.27.
21. *Well Dressed?*, IFM, p.11.
22. Quote from Ineke Zeldenrust of the Clean Clothes Campaign.
23. 'Looking for a Quick Fix', Clean Clothes Campaign, p.12.
24. 'The True Cost of Cheap Clothes at Primark, Asda and Tesco', War on Want, December 2006, p.11.
25. 'Who Pays?', ActionAid, p.32.
26. 'Looking for a Quick Fix', Clean Clothes Campaign, p.71.
27. 'Virtuous Vendors' by Rebecca Taylor, *Time Out* magazine, 11 April 2007.
28. Quoted in 'The True Cost of Cheap Clothing', an *Observer* article, which exposed sweatshop working conditions at the Fortune factory in Cambodia, by Mick Mathiason and John Aglionby, 23 April 2006.
29. Quoted in 'UK Firms "Exploiting Bangladesh"', BBC News, 8 December 2006.
30. A Wal-Mart (the company that owns Asda) spokesperson was quoted in the report 'Fashion Victims: The True Cost of Cheap Clothes' by War on Want, December 2006, p.9.
31. 'Who Pays for Cheap Clothes?', Labour Behind the Label, p.19.
32. 'Trading Away Our Rights: Women Working in Global Supply Chains', *Oxfam International*, February 2004,

pp.44–45.

33. 'Looking for a Quick Fix', Clean Clothes Campaign, p.33.

Chapter 2

1. 'How to Live the Green Life: Part Five' by Julia Hailes, *Daily Telegraph*, 18 May 2007.

2. 'Who Benefits from the Second-Hand Clothing Trade? The Case of Kenya' by Simone Field in final report submitted to ESRC, October 2005, p.2.

3. 'The LMB story', *www.lmb.co.uk*.

4. 'The Impact of the Second-hand Clothing Trade on Developing Countries', Oxfam Research Report, September 2005.

5. 'Can I Give Last Year's Labels to Charity?' by Lucy Siegle, *Observer*, 25 February 2007.

6. Email from Alan Wheeler, 9 February 2007.

7. Textile Recycling Information Sheet, Wastewatch.

8. Email from Alan Wheeler, 9 February 2007.

9. *http://www.worldwar2exraf.co.uk/Online%20Museum/ Large%20photo%20pages/clothingpoints.html*.

10. 'Who Pays for Cheap Clothes?', Labour Behind the Label, 2006.

11. *Well Dressed?*, IFM, p.43.

12. A survey of 2,000 people by Churchill Home Insurance.

13. *Well Dressed?*, IFM, p.14.

14. DEFRA.

15. Wasteguide, *www.wasteonline.org.uk*.

16. ibid.

17. Environment Agency.

18. ibid.

19. 'Fashioning an Ethical Industry', Factsheet 1, published by Fashioning an Ethical Industry, who have produced a range of factsheets for students and tutors.
20. *Well Dressed?*, IFM, p.10.
21. 'If We Make People Think, Then Job Done' by Lisa Armstrong, *The Times*, 9 May 2007.
22. Quoted in 'Carried Away: Hadley Freeman investigates the rise and rise of the "it" bag', *Guardian*, 22 November 2006.
23. 'The Latest Gotta Have It Handbag Can Stop a Train in Its Tracks' by Samantha Thompson Smith, *News & Observer*, 6 November 2006.
24. NPD Group.

Chapter 3

1. *Nylon: The Manmade Fashion Revolution* by Susannah Handley, Bloomsbury, London, 1999, p.45.
2. ibid. p.35.
3. '$10,000,000 Plant to Make Synthetic Yarn; Major Blow to Japan's Silk Trade Seen', *New York Times*, 21 October 1938.
4. *Nylon*, Susannah Handley, p.63.
5. 'Cheap fashion's oily secret', Gossypium newsletter, January 2005.
6. *The Story of Fashion in the 20th Century* by Gertrud Lehnert, Konemann UK Ltd, 2000, pp.56, 72.
7. Main source for this information is *Nylon* by Susannah Handley.
8. *Nylon*, Susannah Handley, p.75.
9. *The History of Pantyhose* by Mary Bellis, available at *http://inventors.about.com /library/inventors/blpantyhose.htm.*
10. *Nylon*, Susannah Handley, p.27.

11. ibid. p.50.

12. ibid. p.27.

13. ibid. p.96.

14. ibid. p.54.

15. ibid. p.80.

16. *Well Dressed?*, IFM, p.13.

17. 'Cheap fashion's oily secret', Gossypium newsletter.

18. *Environmental Assessment of Textiles. Lifecycle screening of the production of textiles containing cotton, wool, viscose, polyester or acrylic fibres*, Laursen and Hanson, Environmental project no. 369, Ministry of the Environment and Energy, Danish Environmental Protection Agency,1997, pp.80–92.

19. 'Transforming the Textile Industry' by William McDonough and Michael Braungart, *green@work*, May–June 2002.

20. Quoted in 'The Plastic Coats with Lots of Bottle' by Ben Rooth, *Manchester Evening News*, 13 March 2007.

21. Comment in *ICIS Chemical Business*, 22 January 2007.

22. 'M&S: The Jolly Green Giant?' by Sarah Chalmers, Edward Heathcoat Amory, *Daily Mail*, 18 January 2007.

23. *Pesticides News* 52, June 2001, pp.12–14. I am indebted to the Pesticides Action Network for much of the statistical information in this section.

24. 'The Deadly Chemicals in Cotton', Environmental Justice Foundation, in collaboration with Pesticide Action Network UK, London, 2007, p.2. North America alone is responsible for 25 per cent of global household cotton-product consumption, and Europe accounts for a further 20 per cent. Demand for cotton is now in excess of 25 million tonnes a year.

25. ibid. p.7

26. ibid. p.34.

27. ibid. p.2.

28. ibid. p.24.
29. ibid. p.16.
30. ibid. p.25.
31. 'A Short History of Denim' by Lynn Downey, Levi Stauss & Co.
32. 'Redressing a Global Imbalance: The Case for Fairtrade Certified Cotton', Fairtrade Foundation Briefing Paper, November 2005, p.2.
33. ibid.
34. ibid. p.3.
35. 'White Gold: The True Cost of Cotton', Environmental Justice Foundation, London, 2005. Uzbekistan is the second largest exporter of cotton, exporting some 800,000 tonnes a year. Europe is the biggest buyer, purchasing a third of Uzbek cotton each year – worth around $350 million (£170 million).
36. 'The Deadly Chemicals in Cotton', Environmental Justice Foundation, p.2.
37. *World Agriculture and the Environment: A Commodity-by-Commodity Guide to Impacts and Practices* by Jason Clay, Island Press, Washington DC, 2004.
38. ibid.
39. *50 Reasons to Buy Fair Trade* by Miles Litvinoff and John Madeley, Pluto Press, London 2007, p.110.
40. ibid.

Chapter 4

1. Quoted by Rowan Garland in BA Hons Course Dissertation, Chelsea College of Art.
2. *An Overview of Textiles Processing and Related Environmental*

Concerns, A.Walters, D. Santillo and P. Johnston, Greenpeace Research Laboratories, University of Exeter, June 2005, p.8.

3. EU Directive 76/769.

4. *An Overview of Textiles Processing*, Walters et al., p.10.

5. *The History of Textiles*, British Textile Technology Group (BTTG), August 1999, p.10.

6. Kate Fletcher's PhD 1999.

7. 'Environmental, Chemical and Factory Minimum Standards for Dyeing, Printing and Finishing Clothing and Textiles', Marks & Spencer Report, November 2006.

8. These carriers can include: halogenated benzenes (bioaccumulatory and toxic); aromatic hydrocarbons (including biphenyls such as 2-phenylphenol); carboxylic acids, including phthalates (DMP, dibutyl phthalate, DEHP), benzoates and alkyl phthalimides, for example N-botylphthalimide.

9. *An Overview of Textiles Processing*, Walters et al., p.18.

10. The EU harmonizing legislation, the 19th Amendment to the Marketing and Use Directive (azocolourants) (2002/61/EC), came into force in 2003.

11. 'Dye Fastness and the Environment: Smart Thinking' by John Mowbray, *Ecotextile News*, April 2007, p.24.

12. 'Better Thinking's Perfect T-shirt, Dyeing for a change: Current conventions and new futures in the textile colour industry' by Cate Trotter, July 2006, p.4. The report is only available online at *http://perfect.betterthinking.co.uk.*

13. ibid.

14. *An Overview of Textiles Processing*, Walters et al., p.13.

15. ibid. p.14.

16. Figures according to UK Trade & Investment, a UK government organization, April 2007.

17. Europe Directive 2005/84/EC.

18. 'Testicular toxicity of di-(2-ethylhexyl) phthalate in young Sprague-Dawley rats' by J.D. Park, S.S.M. Habeebu and C.D. Klaassen, *Toxicology* 171, 2002, pp.105–115.

19. REACH stands for Registration, Evaluation, Authorization and Restriction of Chemicals, which came into force 1 June 2007.

20. 'My Voice: How you can demand better protection of human health and the environment from hazardous chemicals', a Chemical Reaction Report by Madeleine Cobbing, 2007. Chemical Reaction is a joint project of the EEB, FoEE and Greenpeace.

21. ibid.

22. 'Environmental, Chemical and Factory Minimum Standards', Marks & Spencer.

23. ibid.

24. 'My Voice' by Madeleine Cobbing.

25. 'Exponential increases of the brominated flame retardants, polybrominated diphenyl ethers, in the Canadian Arctic from 1981 to 2000' by M.G. Ikonomou, S. Rayne, R.F. Addison, *Environmental Science and Technology* 36(9), 2002, pp.1886–92.

26. *An Overview of Textiles Processing*, Walters et al., p.19.

27. ibid.

28. 'Toxicological profile for chromium on CD-R', ATSDR, Agency for Toxic Substances and Disease Registry, US Public Health Service, 2000.

29. DEFRA Statistics on imports made into UK Ports of Entry for 2006, provided by DEFRA press office.

30. TRAFFIC analysis based on UN Comtrade and FAOSTAT databases, 2006. TRAFFIC is a Wildlife Trade Monitoring Network, a joint programme of the WWF and the World Conservation Union (IUCN).

31. UK National Wildlife Crime Unit, March 2007.
32. CITES is the 'Washington' Convention on International Trade in Endangered Species of Wild Fauna and Flora, and was set up to protect certain plants and animals by regulating and monitoring their international trade to prevent it reaching unsustainable levels. CITES regulates international trade in over 33,000 species (of which approximately 28,000 are plants).
33. CITES UK Implementation Report 2000.

Chapter 5

1. 'Organic Cotton Market Report: An In-depth Look at the Growing Global Market', Organic Exchange, Spring 2006.
2. 'Introducing GS Sustain', Goldman Sachs report, June 2007, page 1.
3. Quoted in 'Fashion with a Heart' by Jenny Levin, *Harper's Bazaar*, August 2005.
4. Information kindly provided by the Labour Behind the Label project. Special thanks to Hannah Higginson and Liz Parker.

Chapter 6

1. '2007 Organic Cotton Report' by Simon Ferrigno, with Alfonso Lizarraga, Prabha Nagarajan and Silvere Tovignan, Organic Exchange, June 2007, p.3.
2. Organic Exchange is a California-based platform that brings together buyers, farmers, NGOs and other stakeholders to help develop and promote organic cotton.

3. 'Sowing the Seeds of Change: Weaving Innovation and Integrity into Organic Agriculture', Organic Exchange, 2006.
4. 'Organic Cotton Market Report: An In-depth Look at the Growing Global Market', Organic Exchange, Spring 2006, p.2.
5. Quoted in 'Back to Basics' by Lynda Grose, *Ecotextile News*, May 2007, Issue No. 4.

Chapter 7

1. Quoted in 'Sweating over sweatshops: supporting "clean clothes" campaigns to end the extreme exploitation that pervades the textile industry is not as simple as just picking the "right" brand to buy' by Mark Engler, *New Internationalist*, November 2006.
2. Unfortunately, the results of WRC's calculations highlighted the stark contrast between living wages and actual wages. In El Salvador, the prevailing wage was $163 (£80) per month, or $0.87 (£0.42) an hour, whereas WRC argued that it would need to be $482.67 (£237.16) per month or $2.52 (£1.24) an hour.
3. 'The Fairtrade Mark: Guide for Certification of Cotton Products', Fairtrade Foundation, June 2006, p.4.
4. *Well Dressed?*, IFM, p.10.

Chapter 8

1. From 'Stella McCartney follows her principles: New fragrance uses only organic ingredients and was not tested

on animals', *Standard*, 13 September 2003.

2. *Let My People Go Surfing: The Education of a Reluctant Businessman* by Yvon Chouinard, Penguin, New York, 2005, p.78.

3. Text based on a profile by Matilda Lee that appeared in the *Ecologist*, December/January 2007.

Chapter 10

1. *Yeah, I Made it Myself: DIY Fashion for the Not Very Domestic Goddess* by Eithne Farry, Weidenfeld & Nicolson, London, 2006.

2. 'Carrying Conviction', *SocietyGuardian, Guardian,* 16 May 2007, p.9.

3. 'The Waste Land' by Jonathan Watts and Jess Cartner-Morley, *Guardian,* 31 March 2007.

4. *Shopping for Vintage: The Definitive Guide to Vintage Fashion* by Funmi Odulate, Quadrille, London, 2007, and *It's Vintage, Darling! How To Be a Clothes Connoisseur* by Christa Weil.

5. *Well Dressed?*, IFM, p. 41.

6. 'Pieces of Me' by Julien MacDonald, *G2, Guardian,* 16 April 2007, p.14.

Index

Acknowledgements

My biggest thanks goes to Laura Sevier for all her research for this book. Without her I couldn't have done it. I would also like to thank everyone at the *Ecologist* for giving me the opportunity to delve into the world of eco fashion.

Executive Editor: Sandra Rigby
Managing Editor: Clare Churly
Deputy Creative Director: Karen Sawyer
Illustrator: Gina Adams
Jacket illustrator: Justine Formenteli, The Art Market
Page make-up: Dorchester Typesetting Group Ltd
Production Controller: Simone Nauerth